PROTEST WITHOUT ILLUSIONS

VERNON RICHARDS
Afterword by GILLIAN FLEMING

*It is not enough to ban nuclear weapons,
If you ban nuclear weapons completely, and even
destroy all the existing stock they will
be manufactured if war breaks out . . . We must
work towards some system which will prevent
war. It requires a different imagination,
a different outlook and a different way of
viewing all the affairs of men from any
that has been in the world before.*

BERTRAND RUSSELL (1959)

*Every generation laughs at the old fashions,
but religiously follows the new.*

HENRY DAVID THOREAU (1817-1862)

LONDON
FREEDOM PRESS
1981

*First published
1981
by FREEDOM PRESS
84b Whitechapel High St
London E.1.*

©*Vernon Richards and
Freedom Press*

ISBN 0 900384 19 0

To my friend
HANS DEICHMANN
whose practical support
has made possible the
publication of this volume

CONTENTS

PREFACE v

1955 Introduction
  H-Bomb (Made in Britain)   1
  Vested Interest & the Bomb   4

1958
  "Nuclear War Means Death"   7
  Resist War!   11
  Aldermaston & After   15

1959
  Swaffham Demonstrations   19
  Germs for Peace!   23
  Imprisonment & Compromise   28
  Peace by Legislation or Direct Action?   31
  Which Road from Aldermaston?   35
  The Question: How would we Ban the Bomb?   41
  Reflections on Capitalism and War   46
  The Labour Party's Damp Squib (on Nuclear Disarmament)   49
  Disarmament? (The Khrushchev-Eisenhower Summit)   52
  Who's Bluffing? (The MacMillan Mission to Moscow)   56
  (The Diplomatic) Carpet Baggers on the Move   60

1960
  Is Power Politics a Hoax?   64
  Is Aldermaston Enough?   67
  (Blue Streak Missiles and) The Crazy Reality   70
  War or Civil Disobedience?   72
  (The Labour Party Conference) And now What?   75

1961
  Sit-Down Without Illusions   79
  (The Sit-Down) Dress Rehearsal or Show-Down?   84
  On the March   89
  (The Communists Join the March) A Welcome to All . . .   93
  The People in the Street   95
  Away from the Parties   100
  War by Accident?   105
  Are our Leaders Suicidal Lunatics?   109

Leaders and Lunatics   112
Solidarity Wanted for Schoenman and Clark   117
Wethersfield Sit-Down   120
Inquest on the Sit-Down — I   122
II — Must We Fill the Prisons?   127
III — Openness or Secrecy?   133

1962-1963
Marching On!   140
Aldermaston 1963   142
RSG-6: Facts and Opinions   146
Reflections on FED 0101   148
The Press Revives the Anarchist Bogey   151
What is CND for?   154

1964
CND Doublethink   157
Reflections on a Committee of 100 Statement   160

Afterword by Gillian Fleming   163

Index   167

ILLUSTRATIONS
©Vernon Richards

I. ON THE MARCH *between pages 32 and 33*
II. FACES AND FASHIONS *between pages 64 and 65*
III. SITTING DOWN *between pages 96 and 97*

> "Incidentally, it was one of the warming and exciting sights of the sit-down demonstration that it was not a blancmange of humanity but a turbulent sea of faces, young and old, smooth and wrinkled, smiling and serious, tense and carefree; each declaring his individuality and at the same time wanting to be, and accepting the responsibility of being, a link in that chain of solidarity and protest."
>
> FREEDOM (March 4 1961)

AUTHOR'S PREFACE

This volume has been compiled with a new generation of anti-nuclear war protesters very much in mind. It is in no way meant to be a history, though it includes first-hand accounts of a number of the Marches and Sit-Downs in the late '50s and early '60s, as well as articles based on Parliamentary debates on "Defence", and on Labour Party Conferences, the relevance of which to the contemporary scene does not, I hope, need underlining. Indeed there are a whole number of parallels that can be drawn, starting with the fact that the Tories were in office for thirteen years, from 1951-64 while the Labour Party was, "as usual", according to Fleet Street, "tearing itself to pieces" in spite of the fact that then the NEC and the Trades Union bosses were on the Right and the protesting minority on the Left. It would be interesting to learn from the Capitalist Press' pin-up lady, Shirley Williams, in what way the present NEC is more intolerant than the one led by her namesake the National Agent Len Williams some of whose utterances are recorded here (see pages 75-78) at the 1960 Scarborough LP conference, when, just as in 1980, the bloc votes of the Unions were tilting the scales in favour of unilateralism. It is also interesting to recall that the Social democrats' guru Hugh Gaitskell remained in the party and successfully manoeuvred the bloc votes to reverse the unilateralist vote at the 1961 conference, just as a number of Party and Union leaders are now seeking to do in time for the 1981 conference.

Such is the political circus and those who feel that by engaging in it they are getting somewhere will obviously not be convinced by anarchist arguments to the contrary. Yet I would still ask them: What can the revived CND expect from a Labour Party in opposition led by Michael Foot which its predecessors could not get from three Labour governments between 1964 and 1979? Two admittedly with small majorities, but in 1966 Labour had a bigger majority than Mrs Thatcher now enjoys.

Neither should one forget that in 1945 with an overwhelming majority, a war weary world, with tens of millions of lives lost, whole regions devastated, the Labour government did nothing to end the arms race. Quite the contrary. In 1955, when Churchill was back in Office, he could justify the *H-Bomb (Made in Britain)* (see page 1) without contradiction from the Labour benches when he declared

Fortunately executive action was taken by Mr Attlee to reduce as far as possible the delay in our nuclear development and production. By his initiative we have made our own atomic bomb. Confronted with the hydrogen bomb, I have tried to live up to Mr Attlee's standard.

Things have not changed. One has only to listen to Question Time in Parliament where the Prime Minister and other Ministers never bother to answer questions put to them by the Opposition. They simply remind them of what *they* did when in Office.

Yet another parallel between past and present is the "imminence of a nuclear holocaust". In 1958 the rallying cry was that "Nuclear War means Universal Death" and all the experts and well-meaning intellectuals were convinced that we were on the brink. In 1980, Professor E.P. Thompson one of the bright young Oxbridge Marxists of a very orthodox *New Left* in 1959-60, is now arguing in *Protest and Survive* that he has

> come to the view that a general nuclear war is not only possible but probable and that its probability is increasing. We may indeed be approaching a point of no return when the existing tendency or disposition towards this outcome becomes irreversible.

The grounds on which he bases his pessimism are "tactical" and "strategic". By tactical he maintains that "the political and military conditions for such a war exist now in several parts of the world" and that the "proliferation of nuclear weapons will continue, hastened by the export of nuclear technology to new markets". Serious as this may be he looks upon the *strategic* "as the gravest" of the two considerations. And for the reason that

> They rest upon a historical view of power and of the historical process, rather than upon the instant analysis of the commentator on events.

For a non-Marxist it is difficult to understand why, in the circumstances, Prof Thompson, should even bother to protest, let alone protest *in order to survive!* Nor will I attempt to summarise his three pages of analysis in which he seeks to show how "deterrence" has wormed its way into the very fabric of society. I feel that some readers will share my despair when I declare that these Marxist *gurus* speak a language which we well intentioned protesters simply cannot understand. I quote:

> 'Deterrence' is not a stationary state, it is a degenerative state. Deterrence has repressed the export of violence towards the opposing bloc, but in doing so the repressed power of the State has turned back on its own author. The repressed violence has backed up, and has worked its way back into the economy, the polity, the ideology and the culture of the opposing powers. This is the deep structure of the Cold War.

Well! If only I could understand that lot I might even tackle — a Blake poem later — Professor Thompson's declaration that "Mystery envelops the operation of the technological 'alchemist'. 'Deterrence' has become normal, and minds have been habituated to the vocabulary of mutual extermination. And within the normality, hideous cultural abnormalities have been nurtured and are growing to full girth" and so on and so on.

It must surely come as an anti-climax for some of his followers when at the end of it all he writes: "I am reluctant to accept that this determinism is absolute".

And our reluctant Professor who sees that some situations are less determined than others then launches his appeal against the logic of his argument

> We must throw whatever resources still exist in human culture across the path of this degenerative logic. We must protest if we are to survive. Protest is the only realistic form of self defence.

Without for one moment wishing to minimise Professor Thompson's good intentions, I find his Marxist logic no less "degenerative" than the one he exposes. After all how can one argue the Marxist deterministic logic for three pages and then accuse the others with their "deterrent" logic of engaging in a kind of brainwashing? Or to explain the "historical view" etc then say "I am reluctant to accept that this determination is absolute" and follow this up by suggesting that "protest is the only form of civil defence"?

This volume of articles, first published in the anarchist journal FREEDOM could well be described in Prof Thompson's words as "instant analysis of the commentator on events" since they were in fact written as the events unfolded and are now published unedited. I am convinced that if one generation can communicate to the next its thinking without the advantage of hindsight, something can be learned which would be lost with editing or rewriting. That excellent writer on "Alternatives" in the *Guardian* reminded us only the other day that "news has a short shelf life. After a week even the Budget goes stale". Is it because so much is happening or because nothing is happening and it is in the interest of the Mass Media to encourage us to discard yesterday's news as irrelevant? A kind of built-in obsolescence of the written word in favour of the news flash!

Is it not of importance to the new generation of protesters that twenty years ago we were being told that the world was on the brink of nuclear disaster, and not only did we survive, but are still unscathed? At the time, those of us who did not accept this brinkmanship propaganda, were pointing out that the war industry was a permanent feature of capitalist economy. This writer was asking in 1962 "Can America Afford to Disarm?"* and his answer was that she could not. At that time no less than 7 million people were engaged in civilian or government programmes. How many jobs in the world today are dependent on "defence" programmes and such institutions as the United Nations? There must be tens of millions of petty vested interests maintaining the cold war and ensuring that it never explodes into nuclear annihilation.

Were I writing today I would add that not only can the industrial powers of the West not "afford" to disarm, but *neither can they "afford" to persuade Russia to disarm*. The so called world recession which all the Western "democracies" blame for their financial crises and mass unemployment just doesn't exist. Industrial production in the world today is greater than it ever was . . . indeed to the point of saturation. Imagine what would happen to world markets if Russia stopped wasting a large proportion of her labour power and resources on "defence". Is it not bad enough to have Japan flooding the world markets with *her* industrial production? Already there are those who are seeking to deal with the Japanese problem by insisting that she should build up her "defence" forces (at present less than 1% of her GNP goes in defence), just as when W. Germany was dominating world markets, the "democratic" powers dropped their plans of keeping Germany occupied and disarmed for at least 50 years, and insisted that she too should join the arms race.

It is interesting to compare the Khrushchev initiative for "total disarmament" (pp.52-55) in 1959 with Breschnev's overtures to the Reagan administration. One can doubt the sincerity of the approach, but when in all

*FREEDOM 17/3/62.

these years have the Western industrial powers ever approached Russia about disarming? And if one may state the obvious, is it not significant that the first thing both Mrs Thatcher and President Reagan did when they took office was to announce massive cuts in public services and more funds for "defence", to the accompaniment of an anti-Russian campaign unequalled in the past 20 years.

Two important articles by Jonathan Steele* on the economic situation in Russia help to confirm my thesis. Our politicians and industrialists must surely shudder at the thought that

The Soviet Union is running into labour shortages. As a general rule it is short of workers with enough skills to make the investments of the last few years pay off in higher productivity. In specific places, such as the whole area east of the Urals which is becoming the new focus of industrialisation, the country is even short of unskilled workers.

Mr Steele refers to the outpourings of Richard Pipes, chief Soviet analyst in Reagan's National Security Council who recently stated that the Soviet standard of living is not higher than 70 years ago, as absurd. He writes

The huge improvements in housing and industrial consumer goods and the lesser improvements in diet are there for all to see. The Soviet Union has not fulfilled Khrushchev's inflated boasts, but its industrial output is 80 per cent of the United States' and its national income two-thirds. Transcaucasia and Central Asia which were relatively untouched by Tsarist Russia have been modernised beyond recognition.

Without suggesting that the Military lobby in Russia is any less determined than its counterpart in the West in protecting its vested interest in the cold war, it is surely obvious however that whereas the Russian economy could make considerable progress if the arms race were to be ended, the same could not be said of the Western Capitalist powers.

Twenty years ago the development of nuclear power stations was in its infancy, and laymen such as this writer were unaware of the environmental and other hazards. We saw in its development the liberation of the coal miner. If I were writing today I would be arguing that the development of nuclear power stations is the greatest of all threats to mankind. The dangers are real, proven, and are already affecting peoples lives and the environment. Whilst I can understand that a new generation sees the H-bomb race, the setting up of missile sites in Europe, and the war-dances of Thatcher and Reagan as issues to protest about, just as twenty years ago it was Polaris nuclear submarines and Blue Streak Missiles, and the "four minute" warning of annihilation that launched the first CND, nevertheless it seems to me that it is the anti-nuclear power station protesters throughout the Western world who are growing in numbers and determination, supported by convincing arguments and alternatives to nuclear energy who give this OAP (Old Age Protester) real hope that something positive may eventually emerge.

Colchester March 1981   **V.R.**

*in the *Guardian* 9-10 March 1981.

1955
INTRODUCTION

H-BOMB (MADE IN BRITAIN)

Two days after the Government's statement that in the next ten years twelve Atom Plants would be built to produce electric power came the announcement that Britain was to develop and produce thermo-nuclear weapons, which include the hydrogen bomb. The timing of the announcements may have been a mere coincidence, and certainly, to judge by the reaction of the Press to this H-bombshell, it might well have been. We are told that the Power plants will involve an expenditure of £300 millions over a period of ten years, but no indication as to how many more millions will be added to the present expenditure of £1,500 millions per annum on cold war preparations (or £15,000 millions in the ten years in which a mere £300 millions are being spent on peaceful uses of atomic energy).

For those people to whom the news may bring "a sickening, sinking feeling" the *News Chronicle* offers the reassuring pill that

we shall be most exposed to the risk of war when we are weakest, and best protected against that risk when we are strong enough to make an attack on us manifestly unprofitable.

The H-bomb, declares the *Evening Standard*, is conceived not as a weapon of attack nor of defence but "as the weapon of prevention". It is "The great deterrent" declares the *Standard* echoing the governmnent White Paper — as presumably the hangman's noose is the "deterrent" to murder?

We are assuming that the Government has not already reached an advanced stage in the production of the H-Bomb, though it would come as no surprise to us to be told, on the eve of some International Congress or other in the near future, that Britain had her H-Bombs all ready for delivery except for the label. On the first assumption, however, Russia and the United States are at present the only two Powers in the world to possess the H-Bomb. We have, furthermore, the assurance of the American Secretary of Defence that "there is no atomic stalemate with the Soviet Union because the United States is out ahead" (*New York Times* 16/2/55). From a military — and, in 1955, political — point of view Russia has only superiority over America in the "conventional" weapons of warfare. And neither Britain nor America are taking steps to achieve parity in this field. Obviously Britain could not and Western Europe will not; only America could but does not. Why?

Perhaps the answer is political and unconnected with purely military strategy. That is, a question of power politics. Let us examine the implications of Britain's decision to make the H-bomb. As matters stand at present, in the event of war Britain will be, as America's European Formosa, the launching platform for the H-bomb attack on the enemy, and will therefore have access to more H-bombs than she could produce herself (quite apart from the ones she will receive in return from the enemy). The decision to produce the H-Bomb cannot, in the circumstances, be viewed, or the expense justified, on military grounds.

Thus so far as Britain is concerned the addition of a made-in-Britain H-Bomb can be explained away neither as a deterrent — for the Americans declare they are "out ahead" of Russia in these weapons, and there is no reason to suppose that they lack the technological and productive capacity to remain "out ahead" — nor on military grounds since, in the event, they will be at the delivering (and receiving) end of all the H-Bombs they want. There can only be one other reason — the political one.

Now it is significant that, whilst America is prepared to supply this country with H-Bombs in the event of war (the least they could do, some would say, in view of the fact that they have established their bases on these islands), they are no more prepared to supply this country with information on their production than they are to Russia. As the *Manchester Guardian* (18/2/55), in a most understanding editorial on American reluctance in these matters, points out:

> The mood of Congress is not towards closer alliance but away from it, as support for the Bricker Amendment has shown. That mood is probably a fair reflection of American feeling. Besides the American Service Departments — not least the Air Force — are distrustful of the British.

But with all its understanding the *Manchester Guardian* adds that in the "hydrogen age" it is "senseless" from the point of view both of America and Britain that the latter should "spend such enormous sums of money" and "devote such great resources to duplicating American efforts" for "each partner is denied many fruits of the other's knowledge. Each is wasting money and technical manpower which could be saved". However, if that is America's attitude, concludes the *Manchester Guardian*, then "the main British decisions (to produce the H-Bomb) appear sound".

To our minds the operative word in the *Guardian's* argument is "partners". We have never taken the view that America and Britain were "partners" in the game of power politics. Let us put it this way. Britain's role as a first class power has in the past depended on the fact that she has been the exponent *par excellence* of the political strategy known as the Balance of Power. With it she has divided the world, Europe and individual nations, her technique being the fostering of national, racial, economic or religious antagonisms, wherever they suited her ends. When in the Europe of post-World War I France's dominant role (followed by the Franco-Russian alliance) threatened the European balance of power, Britain championed the re-emergence of Germany under Hitler and was openly hostile to France; and when, later, Hitler threatened, Britain was once again the friend of France and of democracy.

But Britain emerged from World War II as a second class power. Politically Russia was the strongest force in the world in spite of the Americans' Atom Bomb, and, irrespective of any ideological reasons, Britain's logical place was alongside the United States. But today the roles have been reversed. The United States has become the foremost *world* power, economically, militarily and politically, with Russia (probably still the dominant force in Europe) taking second place. Britain's role is clear. She is a "partner" where it concerns the re-armament of Europe, for there Russia is the dominant power; was a half-hearted "partner" in the Korean venture, and now makes it quite clear that she is not prepared to join the United States in the defence of the off-shore islands of China which, if not strategically important to the defence of Formosa, are nevertheless declared to be of importance to the "fighting morale" of America's ally Chaing Kai-shek. Britain is obviously much concerned with the United States' Pacific defence perimeter, and that country's potentially dominating role in Far Eastern politics, but can at present do little about it. Power politics is hardly disturbed by the "prestige" of a Churchill or the "moral" pressures of a Nehru. So Britain is building her own H-Bombs . . . and then there will be three!

(February 26, 1955)

VESTED INTEREST AND THE BOMB

Much of the 252 columns of Hansard taken up by last week's debate in the House of Commons reads like some surrealistic fantasy by Lewis Carroll, with the difference that the Debate was fantastic reality. That the people of this country place confidence (and their lives) in the hands of the government and their "representatives" can only be explained by the fact that very rarely do they undertake to read the full report of a debate, contenting themselves with the high-spots selected for them by the daily Press, more often than not coloured by the particular newspaper's opinions and personal dislikes. The real issues in the debate, concerning the military policy of this country have been completely swamped by the "Bevan-Attlee struggle". Yet Mr Bevan's contribution occupies only nine columns of Hansard out of 252 and, what is more, his speech occurred late in the debate when other Labour Party speakers had already asked questions similar to the ones he was to ask. But the Press' spotlight was directed on Mr Bevan for reasons which are not difficult to seek.

The debate was, as are all such debates, notable for the accusations and counter-accusations hurled at Ministers by ex-Ministers and *vice versa*, each attempting to justify his actions when in office, blaming his successor or predecessor depending whether he was out of office or in. Even when they discuss the Hydrogen Bomb these petty men seem more concerned with personal vanity than the issues at stake; with scoring party points than with establishing the real facts.

But, as we are always trying to stress in commenting on such debates, they carry little weight, for the decisions have already been made before the debates take place. As Sir Winston pointed out at the beginning of his speech:

> What is the present position? Only three countries possess, in varying degrees, the knowledge and the power to make nuclear weapons. Of these, the United States is overwhelmingly the chief. Owing to the breakdown in the exchange of information between us and the United States since 1946 we have had to start again independently on our own. Fortunately, *executive action* was taken by Mr Attlee to reduce as far as possible the delay in our nuclear development and production. *By his initiative* we have made our own atomic bombs.
> Confronted with the hydrogen bomb, *I have tried to live up to Mr Attlee's standard. We have started to make that one too.* It is this grave decision which forms the core of the Defence Paper which we are discussing this afternoon. (Our italics.)

Faced with the *fait accompli* there was little argument on the question of the merits of producing the bomb. Sir Winston himself seemed to be of the opinion that it was not only a "deterrent" so far as Russia was concerned but would help in Britain's dealings with the United States :

> Personally I cannot feel that we should have much influence over their (the United States) policy or actions, wise or unwise, while we are largely dependent upon their protection. We too must possess substantial deterrent power of our own.

Where there were marked differences of opinion was on the role to be assigned to the conventional weapons of warfare and to the Army, Navy and Air Force in this era of nuclear strategy. Some Members echoed the views of Captain Liddell Hart that all the existing ideas on the Services and weapons were obsolete. But as he pointed out in a *News Chronicle* article (1/3/54):

> The new situation will not be easily accepted. Vested interests are sure to oppose any replanning and re-distribution that follows out the logical conclusion. The reluctance of these interests will be reinforced by a cautious reluctance to abandon any familiar form of defence — even though these provide no real safety.
>
> I can well understand such hesitation to accept the logic of the atomic era. After devoting 40 years to the study of warfare, it is not easy to face up to the fact that this accumulated knowledge has become useless.

The Labour ex-War Minister, Mr Strachey, said much the same thing:

> I was arguing that the role of the Services had been altered. The White Paper says that it has not been. If hon. Members opposite really think that the invention of the hydrogen bomb has made no radical change in the role of the Services, I find it very difficult to believe that I can open their minds to reason at all.
>
> What does that preposterous sentence really mean? It means that the great military interests are still writing White Papers and Defence Estimates — and they are vested military interests. I do not want to attack them; in many ways they are perfectly legitimate and natural interests.

But he went on to deplore the fact that apparently not even the hydrogen bomb could "shift the dead weight of military tradition" even though as another member reminded the House the U.S. experiments had shown that "a battleship can be plucked out of the sea, thrown in again on its stern, turned over and sunk" by the H-Bomb!

There was however, a large measure of support for retaining the military set-up in Western Europe even though there was no intention — or hope? — of being able to match Russian strength in equipment or man-power. The question then arose as to the meaning of the word "aggression" in paragraph 19 of the White Paper which reads: "The knowledge that aggression will be met by overwhelming nucler retaliation is the surest guarantee that it will not take place".

Did it mean, asked a number of Labour MPs, that aggression

with conventional weapons would be met with nuclear retaliation? Some said yes, others said wait and see. But neither the Government nor Mr Attlee (for the Opposition) said "No!" This question was a blow below the belt for if the would-be aggressor were told that any attack would be answered with a few H-Bombs then what would be the advantage of launching his attack with conventional weapons, since he would be giving the other side the opportunity to strike the first crippling nuclear blow which might make retaliation impossible? So the "deterrent" effect of the H-bomb becomes very slender indeed since there is no way of preventing an aggressor from dropping the bombs except by becoming the aggressor and dropping them before he does! And how, and who is, to determine when the other side is about to become the aggressor so as to forestall him?

One Labour Member, Mr Healey, suggested a way out of this very ticklish problem:

> If there is an advance by the Red Army we shall have to drop bombs on the Red Army wherever it may be. My point is that it is surely better, if bombs are to be dropped, to drop them only on the Continent, and not on Britain and on the United States and the USSR. That is something, I should have thought, that we should have been agreed about. (Laughter.) I ask hon. Members to think twice before laughing about this.

One cannot imagine that the French or German people who would be at the receiving end of these bombs would find the suggestion a laughing matter. (But then perhaps we have almost reached the stage where such a proposal might well be considered "inspired statesmanship" on the grounds that only 100 million people would thus be slaughtered, as against the whole of humanity in an "all out" nuclear war.)

We think the H-Bomb propaganda is having the serious effect on the public of confusing the means with the ends. The politicians are trying to make us believe that war or peace are dependent on the H-Bomb. But weapons are in fact still the *means* for waging wars, not the *causes* of war. The causes are still *power politics*, vested interests, slumps; causes which, we will go on repeating, existed before Hitler, before Stalin. Power politics is as much the vice of democracy as of the totalitarian regimes and is at the very foundation of the class society. War is an integral part of such a society.

The menace to world peace is not the Hydrogen bomb but the structure of our society and it is this that needs to undergo revolutionary changes if we wish to banish the horrors of war from the face of the earth.

(March 12, 1955)

1958

"NUCLEAR WAR MEANS UNIVERSAL DEATH"

Alone, among last Sunday's newspapers, *Reynolds News* gives a front page splash to the announcement that "all-out efforts (are) to be launched by MPs, writers and scientists to rally public opinion against nuclear war preparations".

Bertrand Russell is reported as saying that he wants to see Britain adopt the slogan "Nuclear war means universal death", and that if international agreement on atom war cannot be achieved, "then Britain should renounce it unilaterally". J.B. Priestley who, the report continues, "has spent the last few weeks in talks with scientists who will play an active part in this attack on the use of nuclear arms" declared:

> Nuclear war is war against the human race. It is not war as it used to be. It is suicide. In no circumstance should this country use any nuclear weapon, even for defence.

Besides the writers, there is a group of some 20 Labour MPs calling themselves the Labour Party's Hydrogen Bomb Campaign Committee who are "determined to outlaw nuclear war". And there are two groups of scientists in this country "who have set themselves up as watchdogs against possible nuclear dangers. One group, at London University, will keep check on radiation effects on rainwater and foodstuffs; the other is making available to trade unionists and politicians information on nuclear developments".

Finally, it was announced last week "that a conference of top scientists from both sides of the Iron Curtain will meet early in the New Year to discuss ways to ban nuclear war".

A meeting "to decide the best way to organise action" will be held some time this month — according to *Reynold's News* — between the already existing National Council for the Abolition of Nuclear Weapon Tests and the "famous writers and scientists". As vitally interested members of the human race we offer our uninvited views to the meeting.

Before discussing the "best way to organise action" the meeting will, presumably, have to agree among themselves about *what* action they wish to organise. And this, to our minds, will prove the thorniest problem as well as being fundamental to the success or failure of whatever action they may eventually take. The existing National Council opposes Nuclear Weapon Tests. Bertrand Russell and J.B. Priestley go further and call for the abolition of nuclear weapons by Britain, unilaterally if other countries refuse to do likewise. Other participants at the meeting may object, and we hope they do, to the emphasis which both Russell and Priestley seem to place on nuclear war rather than on war itself. Nuclear war "means universal death" (Russell), "is suicide" (Priestley). Indeed Priestley actually says that "it is not war as it used to be". Whilst many of the writers might be prepared to direct their attack on war, the politicians at the meeting may object that total unilateral disarmament would force our Foreign Minister to go naked to future international conferences.

Perhaps the first step should be to discuss the scientific accuracy of Bertrand Russell's proposed slogan "Nuclear war means universal death". If all the scientists are agreed and we have no reason for suspecting their facts and conclusions, then all those gathered at the meeting who cannot accept this should be asked to withdraw. The logical next step for those left is to ascertain if everybody agrees with the Priestley-Russell determination that this country shall abolish its nuclear armament unilaterally if international agreement cannot be reached. Those who cannot agree, yet have previously agreed that nuclear war means universal death, either have the twisted minds of politicians such as Bevan (who one suspects does not imagine that the H-Bomb will ever be used but who, at the same time, thinks that you cannot participate in the international political game unless you possess it) or believe that if Russia is bent on destroying mankind that we should get in first. Such a reaction is as suicidal and neurotic as the third, that Russia is prevented from launching an H-Bomb war by the existence of similar weapons in America and Britain, is unrealistic.

The very existence of the H-Bomb is a threat to mankind; its use, collectively, or unilaterally, by America, Russia or Britain, means universal death; that is, for those at the launching end just as much as for those at whom they have been directed. Thus if any one of the countries possessing H-Bombs were determined to drop them, the possession of even more potent H-Bombs by the others would neither stop them nor could save mankind from being annihilated. To drop more bombs in retaliation would only hasten the process of annihilation.

Our Committee at this stage will divide into two factions. One faction which thinks in political, the other in human terms. Both will be agreed that "nuclear war means universal death" as well as that the threat of universal death can be ended by the abolition of the H-Bomb here and in America and Russia. Those who think in political terms however cannot agree to *their* country making the first move by removing the H-Bomb from *their* armoury and *their* political vocabulary. For them it's either all or nothing, and therefore whatever hopes they have depend on agreement at Top-Level, between politicians, or propaganda directed at the potential enemy countries (surely a proved hopeless task among the unholy trinity?).

Those who think in human terms, who have overcome the obstacles which prevent straight-thinking in politicians, will accept the idea of unilateral abolition of the H-Bomb, and they can now proceed to graft an ethical, a personal meaning onto this slogan — "nuclear war means universal death" — which relies for its strength on Man's fear of death or extinction. To our minds Man spends more hours of his life arguing with his conscience than in thinking of his death* or of the possibilities of his planet going up in smoke (of course it may well be different a hundred years hence when his power of self-destruction is no longer the novelty that it is for us today). And if our committee, that is, what is left of it at this stage, is intent on achieving its ends (and not simply of salving the consciences of its individual members) it must direct its appeal to our "better self"; to something nobler than our narrow self-interest; to something more dignified than our petty (nationalistic) pride; to something more intelligent in us than the standards of our yellow press would lead one to believe. Immediate results might not be spectacular, but at least, so we believe, a minority, a conscious nucleus of determined people would respond, whereas so far, the approach based on fear (after all, we have known of the potentialities of the H-Bomb for years), has not prevented governments from carrying on their lunatic machinations, of digging into the public pocket with impunity, of directing human energy with the self-assurance of slave-drivers, or of talking the most unutterable nonsense which has been lapped up by the philosophers and the in-

---

* One has only to observe the gay abandon with which he crosses a busy road to save perhaps half a minute, or his growing addiction to flying machines and tobacco, to be aware of his contempt for life! And is there no significance in the fact that most young men accept conscription and risk life and limb in war rather than face the hostility, ostracism and imprisonment which are the price they pay for refusal?

tellectuals no less than by the so-called uneducated masses.

For all these reasons we would, as self-appointed chairmen of this gathering of eminent men of letters and science, propose that, whilst in accord with Bertrand Russell's declaration that "Nuclear war means universal death" and with J.B. Priestley's that it is "war against the human race", we should nevertheless not lull ourselves into believing that the removal of the threat of war can be achieved either through sweet reasonableness at top-level or by selling peace with slogans based on fear.

Let us accept, and face up to the fact, that we are at present at the mercy of psychopaths who can press the button which will spell universal destruction. We can do nothing to humour or stop them going their own suicidal way until we (*a*) know what we want (*b*) have crossed the Rubicon, that is, have translated an idea into a desired way of life (*c*) pursue our objective to the bitter end.

We agree with J.B. Priestley when he writes, in his excellent contribution to last week's *New Statesman* (*Utopian Night*) that what is wrong with politicians "and all those closely associated with them" is

their staggering, almost frightening conceit. I remember an editor once telling me that in his view authors and actors, prima-donnas and film stars, and all the other familiar archetypes of human vanity, could not compare in their greed for notice, favour and applause, with most political leaders, whose unwavering rapacity for publicity and praise was almost maniacal. And everything that has happened in our time has tended to increase and strengthen this conceit.

But this is as it should be. The politician wants power just as Imperial Tobacco wants markets. He must convince the public that he knows the answer to every question just as Imperial Tobacco spends millions to convince the public that "Players Please" more than any other cigarette.

What Mr Priestley should investigate more closely is why it is that our writers, our philosophers, our scientists and our "intellectuals" with few exceptions make no impact on the public mind when they lend their names to issues affecting the public conscience and the future of mankind.

(An idea is good or bad irrespective of the moral or spiritual quality of the man who has propounded it. The capacity to translate abstract thought into meaningful words is a great gift but the ideas may be beyond the ability of the writer to live up to *as a person*. This does not affect us if we are influenced by the ideas and not by the personality behind them. But in this age of mass communications, where the writer is — and he has only his own vanity to blame, — if anything, more important than the ideas he expresses, then how he behaves, the relation between what he says and how he acts, between what he said yesterday and what he says today, suddenly loom important. He has, in fact, become a propagandist. Unfortunately our intellectual wants the best of both worlds; he wants both to entertain and be taken seriously; to accept honours and attack class distinctions; to enjoy the advantages of material privilege yet preach material and social equality. Little wonder that their eleventh hour appeals to humanity are received with a shrug and a helpless sigh.)

If mankind is not to be stampeded into mass suicide, we need the modesty and the *sang froid* of starting from the beginning. We must, on the one hand, recognise that the political road only leads to more politics, more conflict and war; on the other that no individual or individuals have the prestige to influence the power struggle between governments, or to halt the development and use of nuclear weapons.

We must reach the people step by step, not by slogans but by awakening understanding in them of themselves and their political and economic surroundings. We must reach them not through fear but through their imagination and aspirations.

Yes, we know that in the meantime we may be annihilated by an H-bomb war. But we should be, in any case, if we went on relying on words without deeds at Top-Level. In any case we are not discouraging the intellectuals from doing what they can; all we are doing is to advise you not to expect more than fine words. Action must, as always, come from below, from you, from us, from the anonymous but real victims who share with the intellectuals the fear of nuclear war but few of their social and economic privileges.

(January 4, 1958)

RESIST WAR!

Next Monday evening at Central Hall, Westminster, the Campaign for Nuclear Disarmament holds its first public meeting. If the distinguished platform succeed in arousing widespread and active interest in, as well as indignation at, the tragic, potentially suicidal, folly of the armaments race they will have achieved something positive. But if, at the same time, they believe that the government (any government) will "follow" the wishes of public opinion, then we believe any good work they may have done will soon be undone. At the Campaign's recent Press conference attended by three members of the Executive, this reliance on action at the top was unfortunately only too evident.

Two members of the Executive also stressed the need for the people to be given "much more information about the threat which armaments represent — especially nuclear weapons". One would have thought enough information had already been given, including the practical effects of such — by 1957 standards mild — weapons as the A-bombs dropped on Hiroshima and Nagasaki not so very long ago, to convince even the dullest mind that nuclear war meant universal death, and prolonged nuclear tests a serious threat to future generations. Indeed, those members of the public who think of these problems are already convinced. They just go on living with the hope that nuclear warface will never take place.

What the people need much more information about are *the causes* of war or war situations, yet on this aspect of the arms race, it would seem that the Campaign has nothing to say. It may be true that the armaments race creates "tensions" between nations (politically speaking, that is) but that is only a by-product, and not the reason for armaments which are but one of the means resorted to for dealing with the *permanent "tensions" that divide the nations of the world*. Wars, and thus armaments, are means to particular ends; they are but the instruments which today, however, have become so effective, so universally deadly, that their use would defeat the ends to which they were put.

Whilst sharing Alex Comfort's view that the world is governed by a bunch of psychopaths, we nevertheless see no evidence to support the view that in pursuit of their quest for power they would resort to means which would utterly and inevitably destroy their ends. Even Hitler, a psychopath if ever there was one, when military defeat was imminent did not resort to germ warfare, though he possessed the means, but instead committed suicide.

The H-Bomb then, has made war, as an instrument of the power struggle, a boomerang, and created a situation in which the weakest power is virtually as strong as those possessing the latest nuclear devices.

In a revealing article in the Sunday *New York Times* (February 1) Walter Millis indicates the *impasse* into which politicians have been led by their own H-Bomb mentality.

> Only recently has the Pentagon come to a serious realization of the extent to which, by staking everything on the threat of instant thermonuclear retaliation, it has paralyzed *any* use of military force as an instrument for the regulation and control of contemporary international relations.

We think members of the Campaign for Nuclear Disarmament would do well to do as we have, and read the foregoing more than once. For in that one sentence are summed up the dangers of war in our society. It has probably already been decided by those in power to ban H-bomb warfare even before public opinion has been organised to actively oppose it, and in spite of the fact that research into the making of bigger and better weapons, and more effective means of delivering them, continues and is ever intensified. War as Mr Millis points out is an instrument for the control and regulation of international relations, and, as we showed in these columns last week, the war industry is a vital safety valve when the capitalist machine threatens to blow up. In a word, capitalism and power politics cannot survive without a cold war economy and force to turn to in periods of crisis. It is not enough, then, for public opinion to be opposed to war — even less if it is opposed only to nuclear war — in order to stop war. The following, in order of importance, are the only positive steps which can lead to the abolition of war:

1. reorganisation of production and distribution on a world scale and based on human needs and not profits.
2. refusal by workers to be employed in industries engaged on war production.
3. mass resistance to conscription, military or industrial, as well as refusal to join Forces on a voluntary basis in spite of financial or other inducements.

We are only too aware of the fact that it is unlikely that any of these steps will be taken in the foreseeable future. Yet there is no easy way round the problem. When Canon Collins CND Chairman said at the Press Conference referred to earlier, that "they were determined to channel the existing feeling in the country and create a climate of opinion which the political parties would have to follow" he was shirking the issue or just using fine-sounding words in which he had little faith. First of all, when he refers to political parties he must either mean the government or nothing at all, since as we are so often reminded it is the government, as the Executive, which determines policy and not the party. Now, the function of the government is to govern, and in this task it has recourse to the Law and to the force behind the Law. To suggest therefore, as Canon Collins does, that we can make the government follow and the public lead is tantamount to putting the government and parliament out of business. This the latter would resist on legal and constitutional grounds and, if it felt the situation called for "firmness", by the use of the police and armed forces, they would undoubtedly be within their legal rights.

How then do Canon Collins and his friends propose to implement the wishes of this public opinion? There can be only one honest answer: by Resistance. If the resistance is to be non-violent then we cannot see how they can advocate anything less than is outlined in our Points 2 and 3 and at the same time appeal in particular to the populations of Russia and America, to follow the example of the people of this island. Paralysis of the war machine in itself might make little difference to the international political situation but the effect on the industrial economy would be immediate and far-reaching, obliging those who are involved in the resistance movement, in their own interest, to extend their activities into the social and economic fields . . . or starve on the dole.

It is, we believe, pretty obvious that the moment you advocate that public opinion should be active as well as vocal you are denying the government its executive powers and admitting that parliament is not the sounding board of public opinion. In a word you are recognising that parliamentary democracy does not work; that is just what anarchists have been saying all along! And because they are realists, as well as human beings, they have been putting forward solutions which, however unattainable they may appear to be to a conditioned, class-ridden, fatalistic and subservient mankind, are nevertheless realistic and practical if mankind really wants all the things, spiritual and material, which it is always saying it wants.

You want peace, you want freedom and security; you need love and you seek happiness; you want leisure and you yearn to be yourself. But you will get nothing so long as you sit back and wait for Big Brother to get them for you!

(February 15 1958)

ALDERMASTON AND AFTER

In a week-end of rain and arctic conditions which apparently set up new records for the time of year, the mile-long file of marchers to Aldermaston was as a warm ray of sunshine penetrating the heavy clouds of mass apathy, mass unimaginativeness and mass defeatism. Even a hard-boiled, cynical press which on Saturday was doing its best to write-off the march as a joke and the marchers as cranks, changed its tune on Monday. Saturday's headline in the *News Chronicle* gloated over the "Heavy fall-out on the road to Aldermaston". Saturday's down-pour seems to have washed the sneer from Mr Barber's lips, and his report in Monday's issue carries the headlines: "Wet and blistered H-marchers are still undaunted". "The freaks and the faint-hearted — he reported — have dropped out, and a thousand or more H-Bomb protesters swung into Reading this evening . . . Few people can be doing this for fun now . . ."

By Monday the march had earned a place in the editorial column. Not of approval, but a sneaking regard for these "few hundred" from a city of many millions who "are seeing the march through" is clearly detected:

Yet this move to renounce Britain's possession of the H-Bomb is by no means negligible. At its lowest it represents a mood that has gripped the population. At its highest it is a sincere attempt to steer a course away from nuclear madness.

In our view the movement has chosen the worst possible course for the best possible motives . . .

To the credit of the marchers and campaigners they have at least made an impression on closed minds. But we do not believe their policy is practical.

The *Manchester Guardian* which headlined its Saturday piece of journalistic whimsy "EARLY DEFECTIONS IN MARCH TO ALDERMASTON. But 2,000 still in the running" on Monday headed the sympathetic report from its special correspondent "PEOPLE WITH A PURPOSE — 1,000 marchers at Reading". What had "started on Good Friday as a Londoner's holiday delight . . . has turned into a recognisable gesture". "The 40 miles since Friday have pared down the march to an assembly of people with some purpose".

The Sunday Press reports we have seen, sobered perhaps by Saturday's rain, were nevertheless coloured by political consideration. The *Sunday Times* headed its report "Disillusion in H-Bomb March", the disillusion, that is, of the "kindly Christian pacifists" who were made aware of the political nature of this allegedly nonpolitical "crusade". According to the *Sunday Times* Fenner Brockway "made the one speech so far which seemed genuinely to try to avoid making political capital out of the march", and their correspondent not only heard a voice crying out in the night (Friday), as the marchers retired to the local church halls, "Tomorrow's *Daily Worker!* Tomorrow's *Daily Worker!*" — a sure sign that the Communists had a finger in the pie* — but he even discovered a live anarchist among the marchers whom he reports in the best Sydney Street traditions of journalism.

> Patrick O'Reilly, an unemployed Irishman, in a knotted red scarf, told me there were ten members of the London Anarchists Group going, as he put it, "part of the way with these people. It's governments who have bombs, and we're against governments".
>
> The Co-operative Party broadcasting van blared out an appeal to "close the ranks, otherwise it looks straggly".
>
> "They want perfection already", the Anarchists grumbled.

(Why is it that for some journalists anarchists cannot talk like other people, or be reported as having "said" this or that, but always "grumble". Is it because they always "see" anarchists talking through their black capes drawn over one shoulder and only revealing eyes alight with murderous intent?)

The *News of the World* with two juicy divorce cases and a further instalment of the memoirs of the naughty Deniza spewing all over its pages, can think up nothing better than "On the Road to Aldermaston" for its short report on the March which, nevertheless, places emphasis on the defections; of the speakers who returned home, of the marcher who "bowed under his rucksack, shook the drops from his umbrella and asked: 'Which way to the station?' Directed, he walked away — to catcalls from his comrades".

The *Sunday Pictorial* true to its unique journalistic formula opens its short, clipped report with "Squelch! Squelch! Squelch! It was a SNIFFLE group which played the anti-H-bomb marchers along the slushy roads yesterday". Only *The Observer's* report combines *atmosphere* with a sympathetic approach to the marchers, and one suspects that Mr John Gale (who writes the report) was a marcher as well as a journalist.

The Aldermaston march was a warm ray of sunshine because it was generated by ordinary people and reached the hearts and minds

---

* It is a fact that by far the most detailed and sympathetic reports published in the daily press appeared in the *Daily Worker* which obviously sought to make capital out of the march even though it does not appear to have been supported by the party members.

According to the *Times'* special correspondent: Suggestions of a political bias in the march have been frequently denied, and one admitted Communist ruefully reflected that there were few present who shared his own ideological viewpoint of other ordinary people along the road from London to Aldermaston and beyond. To our minds this is the positive, practical achievement of the march (apart from the personal satisfaction which those who took part in it undoubtedly derived). The organised "hostility" was far outweighed by the expressions of sympathy and the manifestations of solidarity which the marchers met *en route*. As the *Times* special correspondent reports (April 7):

> As the march has moved westward the attitude of spectators has mellowed. Apart from isolated comments there have been no active displays of hostility, and the number of spontaneous acts of hospitality has increased. The offer of accommodation at the Berry Hill Country Club last night is a case in point, and there was the intervention of a woman, who, on the outskirts of Maidenhead, tossed two umbrellas into the midst of the dripping procession.

It is true that at Twyford a road house owner refused to supply hot water to the marchers to make tea: "To have done so would have meant me losing between £60 to £80 in turnover", he told press reporters. On the other hand at Longford the landlord of a public house supplied them with *free* soup. It is true that the Rural Dean of Windsor and Maidenhead refused accommodation for the night in the church halls because, as he put it "I don't approve of the march". On the other hand, Mr Mark Pick, proprietor of a country club, gave all the marchers coffee, tea, sandwiches, and cakes in a marquee in his club's grounds, provided sleeping accommodation for 75 women and children in the club premises and found accommodation elsewhere for a hundred men marchers.

And what of the confectioner in Slough who distributed bags of sweets and chocolates, and the baker who gave the marchers buns, cakes and rolls; or the householders who offered shelter for the night? In a hundred different ways the bonds of human oneness were forged by the march and obviously meant as much to the givers as to the receivers. In this respect the Aldermaston march was a resounding success.

What a pity the committee did not leave it at that! Instead, as we write these lines we learn that a resolution is to be sent to 10 Downing Street and the United States and Soviet Embassies calling on the respective governments to cease "the testing, manufacture and storing of nuclear weapons immediately". As if governments have a heart or a conscience which can be moved by a thousand, or a hundred thousand, marchers, who instead of spending the holidays at home, at the Zoo, watching football or the changing of the guard, trudge all the fifty miles through snow and rain along A4 to Aldermaston as an earnest of their deepest feelings and sincerity. As if governments which conduct their affairs at "summit level" and impose their policies on the people by the threat of force against whoever dares to disobey, will suddenly change their ways because some, a few, of the people protest.

Not all the marchers were so naive. The *Manchester Guardian* (April 7) reported that:

> Sprinkled more thickly than report has given out are obstinate ones who insist on thinking. An Oxford undergraduate complained of "All this guff about Britain giving a moral lead". He admits the truth of the "moral stuff — but what we want to know is what political action we can take to change the Government's policy even by a little — and nobody here has said a thing about that".

That is a question which neither the political Left nor the allegedly politically uncommitted progressive movements, such as the Peace Pledge Union or the Campaign for Nuclear Disarmament, can answer so long as they continue to use public agitation as a means for changing — or influencing — government.

A future march to Aldermaston will answer that Oxford student's question — or rather will *modify* it — when we make it clear that we march to Aldermaston not as a symbol but the reality; that is, we march to Aldermaston to speak to the scientists, the technicians and the workers engaged on the production of the H-Bomb and not as a gesture which we hope may *move* governments. We shall begin to "influence" governments when we dissuade — or failing that, *prevent* — our fellow beings from engaging in the development and production of nuclear — AND conventional! — weapons.

How to set about this task calls for long and serious discussion and the examination of the armaments industry in all its ramifications. At the same time an effort must be made to reach all workers engaged in that industry and make them conscious of the anti-social nature of their work. (Note: the problem of the workers' "vested interest" in armament production and their resistance to appeals to refuse to engage in this work, exists even if one's appeal is made through the agency of governments.)

The Aldermaston march was a magnificent gesture and a moving protest. Now if we mean business, it is needful to clothe the slogans with action informed by a dispassionate examination of the problem.

(April 12, 1958)

THE SWAFFHAM DEMONSTRATIONS

So far as the popular press is concerned, the release of the imprisoned Swaffham missile base demonstrators is the signal for the curtain of silence to be lowered on the whole affair. Having in the first place been responsible for a demonstration by a hundred people becoming front page headlines throughout the country, Fleet Street also decides when the time has come for the public to forget that it ever occurred. But in the minority press it would seem that discussion has only just started, and while much of it is depressing, one cannot help feeling that the growing scepticism among political parties and leaders, and the growing emphasis placed on individual responsibility, brought out in the course of these discussions will find a response in the heads and hearts of at least a few more people. To our minds, the success of the demonstration as propaganda by example — apart from its importance to the demonstrators personally — does not depend on whether it succeeded in stopping work on the missile bases, but on its impact on individual members of the public.

In a letter to *Peace News*, Bertrand Russell maintains that the demonstration was "abundantly justified" on the grounds that whereas "peaceful and orderly activities by those who hope to prevent nuclear warfare" have been boycotted by the Press, the North Pickenham demonstration "secured wide publicity". He concludes that:

> Those who think such methods undesirable should tackle the Press. Until the Press pursues a wiser policy, it is only by methods such as those used at North Pickenham that public opinion can be made aware of the fact that our population is being led blindfold towards mass extinction.

Bertrand Russell makes an interesting point but he does not in fact tackle the main problem. He complains that

> a large conference of eminent men, mostly scientists, was held in Austria in September . . . and drew up a valuable document signed by all but one of the participants at the Congress (yet) hardly any newspaper in this country said one word on the subject.

As if the Press was a public service and not the property of wealthy groups who besides making money out of the Press use it to further their political and other interests.

Just as the Press splashed the Swaffham demonstration, so might they have relegated it to a paragraph at the foot of an inside page. By saying as does Bertrand Russell that "Direct Action" is justified on the grounds that it gets the headlines, he not only does not face the deeper implications of direct action but also skates over the real problems of the Press. The answer to Press suppression or censorship is a Free Press, and the first step towards the building of a Free Press will be taken when people like Bertrand Russell refuse to write for the gutter press.

The people will only break the stranglehold of the millionaire press by creating their own organs of communication and ideas. Just as we believe that government and centralised authority will be weakened only when we, the people, succeed in creating our own social and economic organisations, and thus remove initiative from the government, so with the Press. Our writers, thinkers, artists, poets and honest journalists on the one hand, and that substantial minority public which is sick and tired of the sensationalist antics of the gutter press on the other, should boycott the gutter press and combine to produce and support a new, a free, Press which extends the freedom of expression to its contributors and takes for granted the intelligence of its readers! It can be done if enough of us wants it *and are also prepared to do something to achieve it*.

The *Socialist Leader* in a recent editorial refuses to be enthusiastic about the Swaffham demonstration. The editorial writer recognises the good intentions of the demonstrators but looks upon them as being "slightly mixed-up". Allowing for the fact that the ILP is a party which suffers from tapeworms* and therefore has a rather sour outlook on life the *Socialist Leader's* criticisms have a certain validity. The first is that the campaign should be directed against "conventional" armaments and the idea of war itself, and not just against rocket bases. They are criticisms we have ourselves levelled at the Campaign for Nuclear Disarmament at various times — the more so since, in our view, a "conventional" war is a much more real possibility in the near future than extermination of the human race by H-Bombs. But we do not feel such criticism has any real bearing on the effectiveness of the Swaffham demonstration. The second point made by the *Socialist Leader* was that the demonstrators in the main were supporters of the Labour Party "and would support a Labour candidate in an election against, say, a member of the ILP".

Now, apart from the fact that the *S.L.* reveals its own interest in

---

* At one time it had to fight a communist fifth column in its midst; later it was the Trotskyists, and since the latter joined the Labour Party it's the pacifists who have been undermining the Party which only asks to be left alone to go through the motions of any self-respecting party aiming at getting candidates elected to Parliament.

votes just like any other political party, its assumptions are wrong. *Peace News* (January 2) publishes the results of a questionnaire completed by 69 of the 100 demonstrators at Swaffham on December 20, showing that whereas only 15 and 5 were supporters of the Labour Party and Communists respectively, 46 were supporters of no party. But when the *S.L.* points out that "pacifists generally" who supported the Labour Party and *Peace News* which carries on "an intense campaign against war, and helps to put people in the House of Commons who are *not opposed to war* . . .", are "mixed-up", they are talking sense, and one hopes that in fact the Direct Action group within the pacifist movement represents the positive protest against not only the "mixed-up" element but also the dead-hand of the respectable sponsors, directors and management committees, as did the Forward Movement in the early months of the 1939 war.

Peace News is at the cross-roads. Our friend, Hugh Brock, the editor, and his assistant Christopher Farley are in prison for their part in the demonstrations, and Michael Randle, chairman of the Direct Action Committee, "has asked to be relieved of his duties in the publishing department, and left *Peace News* last week to take up full-time work with the 'D.A. Committee against Nuclear War'." The Editorial in last week's issue (January 9) "Politics and the Bomb" attacks the Labour Party and exposes the duplicity of Michael Foot and *Tribune* for soft-pedalling the H-Bomb in favour of the Party, but it is clear that the writer still thinks in terms of party politics when he says:

> All pacifists, as well as those who have campaigned for the renunciation of the H-Bomb, have, we suggest, a moral obligation to do what they can to ensure that the issues that they have declared to be of supreme importance shall figure in the forthcoming election.

The *New Statesman* (January 3) in its Editorial "Propagandists and Witnesses" surprisingly dismisses all the "respectable" criticisms of the demonstration and concludes:

> First, there can be no doubt that the 'expediency' wing of the Labour Party has gained a decisive upper hand in recent years, and that with Mr Bevan's defection the 'principle' wing has lost its voice. Second, in the case of the rocket-bases, the constitutional methods of the campaign have been shown to be ineffective: the official Labour line is to oppose the bases, but in practice it has done nothing. The demonstrators can reasonably claim that, the resources of the constitution having been exhausted, they are at liberty to seek others. Third, and most important, is time. Society could afford to take twenty years to end the slave trade. The nuclear holocaust may be lit tomorrow. What drives the marchers down the road to Pickenham is the sound of time's winged chariot behind, trundling its cargo of death.

Fine! But what do the pundits of the *New Statesman* propose as the next step? And what part are they as a journal, and as individuals, proposing to play?

First and foremost the importance of the Swaffham demonstration is for those who actually took part in it. Leaving aside the outside reactions (on the one hand more than 2,000 greetings and presents from well-wishers, on the other the hostility of the workers on the building site, and in the village), those who went the whole hog and, as we write, are drinking their evening mugs of cocoa, and flavouring their "cob" with a microscopic piece of "mouse-trap", far from feeling depressed or regretting their actions will feel the real power that exists within each of us. The power to feel free within the confines of a prison cell; the strength to forego two days' public holiday and tradition in return for the promise of being on "good behaviour" (in the eyes of the law) for one week; the principle of preferring fourteen days behind bars than 365 days *conditional* freedom outside; the sudden awareness that the things that matter most in life are those to which we give least time . . . and *vice versa!*

The lessons of Swaffham are many and we have hinted at but a few. They are tactical and moral. Because we think that the special need today is for us as individuals to put our own houses in order, we have placed more stress on the moral aspects of the demonstration, and we are grateful to these young people who, by their uncompromising actions, not only have made us relive what is, for us, an exciting "past", but have prodded us into looking for an equally exciting future!

(January 17, 1959)

1959

GERMS FOR PEACE!

For the worrying type of person it cannot be said that there is ever a dull moment in the world we live in. Every day the Press provides us with a rich harvest of disasters, tragedies, murders and assaults, not to mention political crises and breath-taking accounts of brinkmanship at top level, which are guaranteed to kill or cure. And what is even more extraordinary is that when one imagines that government-sponsored scientists have plumbed the depths in their search for the last word in the instruments of human extermination, or that politicians have told the biggest lie, perpetrated the greatest injustice ever, or resorted to the most disgusting violence imaginable against their political enemies, one may live to learn that in their quest for power over their fellow beings, there are no limits to what politicians will do to achieve their ends, and, alas, no limits to what some of their lackeys are prepared to do in return for money, success and status.

The atom bombs of Hiroshima and Nagasaki now appear as child's play compared with the potentialities of today's megaton H-Bomb; the V1s and V2s which drove thousands of innocents to their graves and the mental hospitals are mere fireworks compared with the latest fashions in missiles. But though existing weapons are sufficiently powerful to be capable of exterminating mankind, it is the height of political naivety to suppose that politicians will rest satisfied, or that scientists have exhausted their knowledge or their ingenuity. After all the H-Bomb is a cumbersome and complex weapon, and just as "Progress" in aeronautics is measured by the increase of pay-load, as well as of speed, so Progress in death, in mass extermination, will surely be judged both by the speed of extermination and by deaths per bomb-ton. In this respect perhaps we cannot hope for spectacular Progress in the H-Bomb (apart from the method of delivery, and no one can deny that the development of missiles is a big advance on the old-fashioned, conventional, jet-bombers) especially if the scientists' hands are tied by agreements to suspend the testing of these weapons.

But before the public accepts the H-Bomb as yet one more unwanted paid-guest in the family circle, it should be reminded that this is no guarantee that we will not ultimately be saddled with other equally unwanted, "more ultimate" weapons. Of course we have in mind the news released last week that Britain's scientists have produced the last word in germ horrors. At the Microbiological Research Centre and the Chemical Defence Experimental Establishment, scientists are working on 40 or more plague germs, on polio type viruses, nerve gases, cholera and typhus germs. Their crowning achievement is the concentration of Botulinus toxin (which in nature is formed when meat or vegetables are improperly canned) thousands of times more than it is found in nature. Professor E. Maurice Backett, Professor of Social Medicine in the University of Aberdeen, described the effect of these germs in the following terms: "(It kills) principally by paralysing the nervous system. One small teaspoon of the powder contains enough botulinus toxin to kill a million people".

An *Observer* correspondent quotes experts as saying that 8½ ozs. of it "properly distributed would kill everyone in the world". The *News Chronicle* correspondent's authorities are more optimistic and put the quantity required at 16 ozs. In view of the fact that (thanks to the hard work put into the problem by scientists) the concentrate can be mass-produced cheaply, it matters little whether the quantity required is 8½, 16 or 160 ozs. The fact is that we are on the brink of yet another "revolution" in science and who knows, power politics as well. Here at last is the portable mass-exterminator. In years to come, while Foreign Ministers are still busy in Geneva working out a formula for an "effective" control of H-Bomb testing and production, every government will have planted innocuous-looking tourists throughout the world whose suit-cases will have no false bottoms, and whose only knowledge of their surroundings need be the location of the municipal water works. In one waistcoat pocket a miniature receiving set, in the other a phial of Botulinus toxin, such will be the uniform (with seasonal variations of course) and equipment of the armed forces of tomorrow!

A socialist Nuclear Disarmament Campaign supporter with whom we discussed this latest "unseen deterrent", as the *News Chronicle* correspondent so conveniently describes Botulinus toxin, declared that he would not be surprised if governments had been responsible for the publicity as a means of distracting attention from the H-Bomb and the growing public reaction against its continued production and testing. When we argued that to us the new "deterrent" confirmed us in our view that until we campaigned uncompromisingly against *war*, mankind could never be safe from the possibility of extermination by man, he replied that the testing and use of nuclear weapons not only threatened us but also generations yet unborn; that it was one thing to be killed or maimed in war, quite another to be responsible for millions of deformed creatures in generations to come *as a result of our actions now*. This is a very human and generous sentiment.

It is a very unrealistic one too, for it seems to us that we can only protect the interests of those who come after us by succeeding in being the masters of our own destinies in the present. It is surely ridiculous to assume that a government will need the warnings or the protests of people, however eminent they may be, speaking in the name of posterity, but who lack the militancy, the courage to defend human dignity in the present. H-Bomb fall-out will be responsible for physical deformity in generations to come. But what of the social environment into which these future men and women will be born? Surely, those of us who profess to progressive ideas know what this means for us today. What have we done to clear the air for the future?

Botulinus toxin, from the point of view of our socialist friend, must be classified as a conventional weapon in war and power politics. On the one hand, as Professor Backett puts it: "it is now possible for anyone who really wants to, to bump off the human race" (and this, from the point of view of future generations is a much more serious consideration than a few million deformed creatures as a result of H-bomb test fall-out). On the other hand Dr Brock Chisholm, former Director-General of the World Health Organisation, describes B.T. as being capable of killing "anyone who breathes or touches it within six hours. It oxidises within twelve hours, *leaving the area clean for occupation*" (own italics). Which means that future generations are spared (assuming of course that they are ever born), and therefore presumably our socialist friend will not feel called upon to protest against B.T. as he does against the H-B.

Questions have been put to the government about the work of the two establishments referred to which are engaged on germ "warfare". In his reply, the Minister of Supply (and Poison?) said that the Ministry of Supply Establishments "were mainly engaged on research on defensive problems of microbiological chemical warfare".

Mr Jones said most of the results obtained were published in open scientific literature. There was included the botulinus toxin referred to in recent newspaper statements.

This substance had been well-known for many years and the threat posed was grossly exaggerated since the toxin could not be easily disseminated and was not self-propagating. A number of useful defensive measures were known against it.

It was possible that other bacteria or viruses spelt greater danger. The purpose of his establishments was to determine and to reduce those risks, a task in which, in some respects, they had been notably successful.

The establishments, declares Mr Jones, are *"mainly"* engaged on research, etc. It would be interesting to know what they did for the rest of the time. His reference to "research on defensive problems" implies that the government is not interested in the production of the weapons themselves. Yet it is difficult to know how one can do the one without the other.

Dr Chisholm recalled that in 1944 when he was Director-General of Canadian Army Medical Services he took 235,000 doses of anti-botulinus vaccine from laboratories in Suffield Alta to Great Britain.

> It was administered to British, American and Canadian troops, and word of it was "leaked" to German spies so that the Nazis would know the Allies *could also produce bacteriological weapons*" (our italics).

So much for Mr Jones' reassurances about "defensive research". As to the threat being "grossly exaggerated" on the grounds that the toxin could not be easily disseminated, or that a number of useful defensive measures were known against it, Professor Backett thinks differently. When asked "how would it be used as a weapon of war" he replied, unlike the Minister, modestly: "I am no expert on this" but

> I should imagine that an enemy agent would spread it. This could most easily be done by putting the powder in the water supply, say a large reservoir.
>
> A teaspoonful in the water supply of a large city would be virtually undetectable and would remain long enough to do its deadly work of paralysing everyone who drank it.

As to immunisation against it he said:

> In theory, yes. But in practice, no.
>
> There are a number of difficulties. Botulinus exists in various forms and you might go to the trouble of immunising the whole population to one strain and then find they were exposed to another.
>
> In any case, such an immunisation programme could not be hidden from the rest of the world and no potential enemy would think of using the particular toxin against which immunisation had been carried out.

And for good measure he adds:

> Besides, botulinus toxin is a relatively ineffective bacteriological weapon. Much more deadly things exist.

So before Botulinus Toxin Disarmament Committees are formed by well-meaning citizens, remember that Viruses are more deadly than the much maligned Botulinus toxin. Says the Professor:

> Viruses. The bacteriologists have found means of changing relatively harmless virus into virulent, paralysing forms simply by passing them through animals a few times and then growing them.
> Live virus is a much more efficient weapon than toxin, which is a once-for-all affair.
> A virus is self-propagating and once planted in a susceptible population will go on killing until a vaccine can be made against it.
> *Q. Which would be too late?*
> Yes. I am convinced that the bacteriological warfare people now have horrors ready to be used which make botulinus toxin a relatively harmless weapon.
> One of the difficulties of defence against these things is that the research on which they are based is never published.

But Professor, grateful as we are to you for your blunt exposition of the facts, may we suggest that in your conclusion you cannot see the wood for . . . laboratories? And power politics? There is only one possible *defence against these things*. We, you, every one of us who can still think of society in terms of human beings and not systems or power blocs, who can distinguish between human dignity and cheap, ignorant pride, we can offer the only defence against these things: by requesting the scientists manning them to get out, and then smashing these establishments to smithereens so that no one may again use them in our time.

(January 31, 1959)

IMPRISONMENT AND COMPROMISE

Laurens Otter, one of the two Swaffham direct actionists who fasted during their recent imprisonment, asks his anarchist friends what, in their opinion, should be the attitude of anarchists in prison. Should they court discomfort? Should they break the rules and disobey orders and inevitably be punished? Should they behave in a way calculated to upset prison routine as well as the tempers of their "guardians"? Should they refuse to say "Sir" to the Governor and his lackeys, and to take their hands out of their pockets when ordered to do so?

We believe there can be no straightforward yes or no answer to these questions. If we are asked our opinion as to whether an anarchist or any "political" prisoner should accept a "red band", special "privileges" or report fellow prisoners to the authorities, our answer is an emphatic No! If we are asked whether we should protest against the ill-treatment or provocation of fellow-prisoners by the staff, our answer is an emphatic Yes! Again, if we wish to protest against wrongful imprisonment then it seems to us an obvious thing to draw attention to one's case by whatever action we think will serve these ends.

In qualifying our use of the term "wrongful sentence" — all prison sentences are wrong if one is opposed to the penal system — we may also explain why we do not think there is a black and white answer to our correspondent's questions. On many occasions in these columns we have argued that though the system under which we live is immoral by definition, there are moral and immoral ways of behaving within that immoral society. We may not believe in the money system but the shopkeeper who gives the wrong change or the wrong weight cannot be put on a par with the shopkeeper who does not; we may be opposed to the property system, yet does this blind us to the fact that there are extortionist landlords and "fair" landlords? We may be opposed to the system of law but we can still distinguish between its honest and dishonest application. Similarly we may be opposed to the prison system but cannot deny — those of us who have tasted its bitter fruits — that there are those in its service who carry out their jobs in a more humane way than others.

No one in his right senses goes to prison willingly. But revolutionaries of every complexion must approach the possibility of imprisonment as one of the many consequences of their actions. For our part we see no special virtue in "breaking the law" as a principle, just because all laws or rules today are imposed from above. To do so, apart from its consequences in permanently removing us from the outside world, encourages a fanaticism, and a concentration on the Self which may be good for the purity of our souls, but which in the end, however, divorces us from the realities of the social struggle.

We believe that the revolutionary who can hope to make some real contribution to this struggle of humanity for a better world, is the one who sees the problems of society as concerning individuals yet whose actions and decisions rise above the individual self, the ego. For this reason we are always wary of those who are introduced to us as anarchists because they are considered as *individualists*.

We believe that every man should learn to make his own decisions, yes. But we also believe that he should have a breadth of vision, and feeling towards the ideas he seeks to further to make it possible for him to distinguish between those actions which truly serve the cause he has espoused and those which only serve to give him, as an individual, a feeling of satisfaction or self-righteousness. Conscious martyrdom, we think, is an unhealthy manifestation of the latter.

A term of imprisonment, on condition that one sees this curtailment of one's liberty as serving useful ends, can be (if not too prolonged!) for some individuals a valuable experience. It can help one to see more clearly many social problems as well as strengthening those qualities which make up an integrated human personality. We do not think, however, that this is achieved by a calculated attempt to disrupt the prison routine at every turn. (That is, not unless it is a concerted effort by at least a majority of the inmates.) An individual who breaks all the prison rules can hope for neither sympathy from outside or from most of his fellow prisoners nor from his gaolers who are obliged to work overtime as a result. What is important, and a positive achievement, is the ability of the prisoner to broaden his personality, to earn the respect of his fellows and his gaolers by his bearing at all times. One can in fact be uncompromising in prison without breaking the rules.

For many politicians, imprisonment has been a stepping stone to power. There is probably not one nation which has achieved "independence" in these post-war years whose leaders have not served considerable terms of imprisonment. To court imprisonment as a means of shaking the public conscience is a good thing: as a means of furthering the cult of the personality it is harmful. If the result of an individual's imprisonment for breaking the law in protesting against an injustice or for upholding what he considers a fundamental right is that of giving others the strength to do likewise on other occasions, or to provoke reflection among them, away from the traditional patterns, then, to our minds, that action, and the personal inconvenience resulting from it, have been more than worthwhile. If, on the other hand, imprisonment serves only to build up a personality in the mind of the public, then the privations involved have been of no avail — unless, as we pointed out earlier, one happens to be an ambitious politician, in which case they are the very results one was hoping for.

The question our correspondent, Laurens Otter, should ask himself is whether he went to prison to further a cause, to court martyrdom (in the pure, unadulterated, masochistic sense) or to further any hidden or open desire to gain approval among his circle of friends. (As the writer of these lines knows our correspondent only by name we are neither "hinting" nor being personal in our 'reflections'.) To our mind (and we hope we are right), the majority of the Swaffham demonstrators accepted 14 days in prison rather than the alternative of undertaking to be "of good behaviour" for 365 days, for tactical reasons. Firstly, because for a propagandist or 'direct actionist' 14 days in prison is the lesser of the two punishments for their "illegal" actions. Secondly, because as good propagandists they saw the added publicity value as well as the moral impact on some people of being remanded in custody over the Xmas holidays and serving 14 days rather than abandon their plans for more 'direct action' during the next 12 months. In the circumstances the social aspects of imprisonment *per se* were of secondary importance, and one cannot be surprised if the public, and some Swaffham supporters among them, found some difficulty in relating the hunger strikes to the main issue. This is not a criticism of our young friend, who did what he did in all sincerity, without, if one is to judge from his letter, much considered thought. It is simply a point of view informed by some experience of prison and propaganda which we hope may stimulate discussion. And not just for the sake of discussion but in order to propagate more effectively ideas which many of us connected with FREEDOM sincerely uphold as the basis for a new way of life.

(February 7, 1959)

PEACE BY LEGISLATION OR DIRECT ACTION?

The debate in the House of Lords last week on the subject of Nuclear Disarmament contained, besides the expression of personal opinions, much factual information which one would have thought was of vital interest to the people of this country. Brief reports of the debate were published by the Press, but the view expressed by Lord Simon, the proposer of the Motion, in winding up the debate, that he "regarded it only as the beginning of what will be a great debate in the country" was pure wishful-thinking . . . unless something happens very soon to shake the people out of their present torpor. By now most adults in this country and in the rest of the world must have a pretty clear picture of the destructive capacity of an H-Bomb and of the consequences of a nuclear war. They may ignore some of the secondary effects, or not clearly understand some technical aspects of nuclear fission. But they know that nuclear war means annihilation, and this includes themselves and their families and friends as well as their "enemies".

The weakness of their reactions to this knowledge may in part be explained by the very magnitude of the disaster which makes one's personal reaction to it utterly remote and unreal: if everyone is condemned to death then death loses its significance. In any case against whom can one defend one's life since all are condemned to die?

Those nuclear disarmament propagandists who despair at the poor results of their campaign so far, must also recognise that normally healthy human beings are much more preoccupied with the problems of life than with thoughts of death, for life would become intolerable if we allowed thoughts of death to dog our very footsteps. After all, not even the daily Press' catalogue of disaster, of deaths by food-poisoning, in car and air accidents, through leaking gas taps and open fires, seems to deter the majority of human beings from themselves taking risks in their day-to-day lives which a concern with death would make them hesitate to take. Do these reactions show a zest or a contempt for life? Or does it perhaps lead one to believe that though most people are endowed with an animal will to live, few have developed a personal philosophy of life, beyond that of living for the moment?

Such human material is not easily influenced by argument, moral or reasoning, but is obedient to authority, and is conservative. In fact it is just how the Churches and the politicians want mankind to be.

(In spite of all the talking at election time, elections are not won on argument. The country is divided into three sections: the one which always votes for the Conservative, the one which always votes Labour and by comparison to the first two, a small, third section of "floating" voters, fence-sitters or indifferents on whom the parties direct their big-guns not of ideological argument — assuming they had any to offer — but in the form of cheap baits of less income-tax, cheaper homes, penny-off-the-petrol or free wigs.)

We who are propagandists as well as anarchists, carry on our activities in spite of the bleak prospects for change in the immediate future because we have not lost faith in ourselves. The fact that we as individuals can react against the conditioning efforts of mass communications and the social institutions, leads us to believe that others can do likewise. (Only priests and politicians think of themselves as the exceptions to the rule of human stupidity, fallibility and lack of imagination, initiative and responsibility.) What is it that we want to achieve?

In the House of Lords debate on Nuclear Disarmament, Bertrand Russell had this to say:

> We must work towards some system which will prevent war. It requires a different imagination, a different outlook and a different way of viewing all the affairs of men from any that has been in the world before. I believe that war began in Egypt somewhere about 4,000 BC and has gone on ever since, and we have got used to it. We have to get non-used to it, and that it not an easy effort. But we have to make the effort; and those of us who cannot make that effort are contributing their little bit towards the extinction of the species.

These were, to our mind, the most practical words uttered in that debate, for what Bertrand Russell was saying was that nothing in human society is absolute or pre-ordained. The fact that in the past 6,000 years men have resorted to war is no reason why they should continue to do so. After all in those 6,000 years there have also always been men who have defended peace and who have defended freedom of thought.

We anarchists consider ourselves more realistic and in the long run more effective than Bertrand Russell and his friends, when we attack the systems, the thinking, and the values of which war is a by-product, rather than concentrate our arguments and appeals on the *finality*, so far as the human species is concerned, of nuclear war. We *recognise* the possibility that we may be snuffed out in the middle of a sentence of sweet reason and brotherly love by the fall-out of an H-Bomb (of any nationality) released, on the written instruction, of say, even a healthy, British politician — agreed. But we are *convinced* that the threat of extermination by nuclear war

ster 1959. Canon Collins objects to a group
schoolboy protesters who have put
mselves at the head of the March as it sets
from Turnham Green to central London on
last day. Michael Foot looks on, while
rnalist James Cameron is clearly more in-
ested in the young rebels than in their elders.

On the March

3 The editor of t[he]
New Statesman[,]
Kingsley Marti[n]
dispenses the d[aily]
News for Mich[ael]
Foot (left) and [?]
Levy.

4 Finchingfield
village. Assem[bly]
for the Easter
March to Lon[don]

2 Easter 1959. On the march somewhere in Berkshire.

6 Easter 1961. Members of the Tunbridge Wells CND youth group.

5 Easter 1961. Roadside lunch somewhere in Berkshire for members of the Burgess Hill School contingent.

7 Easter 1962. Last day at Turnham Green; the musicians await their cue.

9 Easter 1959. The Steelband lead the African contingent

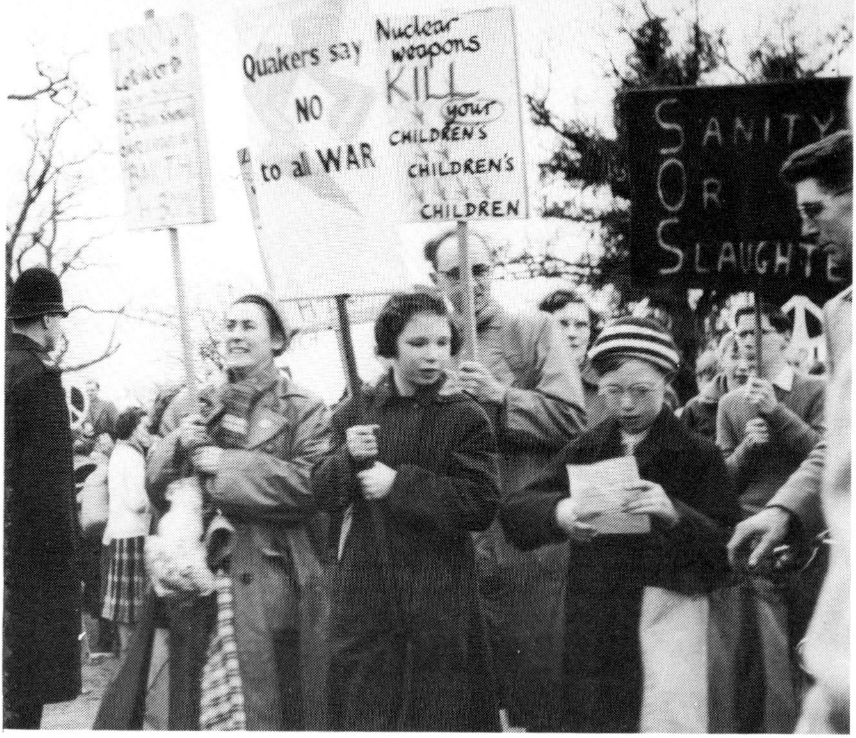
Quakers say
NO
to all WAR
Nuclear weapons
KILL
your
CHILDREN'S
CHILDREN'S
CHILDREN
SANITY
OR
SLAUGHTE

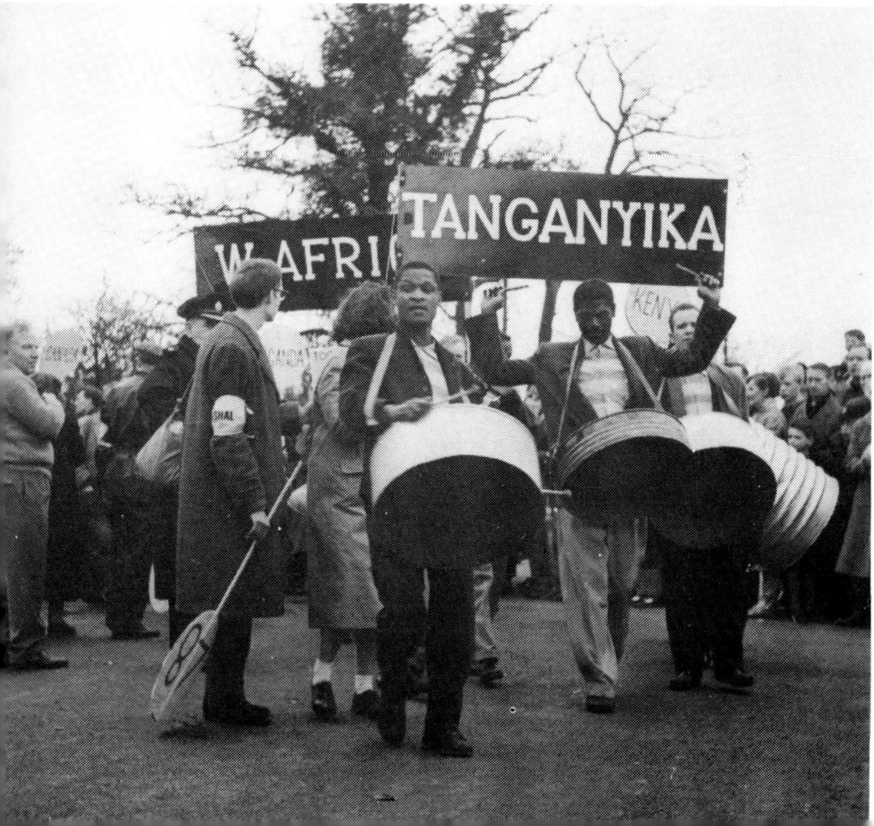
TANGANYIKA
W. AFRI

10 Easter 1960.   Protesters of the 1980s?   **11** Easter 1962.

12 Easter 1961. The young philosopher from Tunbridge Wells.

will not be removed by Act of Parliament! The H-Bomb is a weapon of war in 1959 just as the tank was in the 1914-18 war and the V1s and V2s (not to mention the flame-throwers) were in World War II. The danger it represents exists *because the danger of war exists.* You eliminate extermination of the human race by H-Bombs (and — incidentally — germ warfare as well) not by agreements to ban nuclear weapons but only by abolishing the armed forces, that is, by removing *all possibilities of waging war.* This, Bertrand Russell, unlike many of his friends in the Nuclear Disarmament Campaign, apparently now realises:

> I should like to say a little about the larger context in which I see this Motion. I regard it as a first move, and I hope a practical move, in a long campaign. The long campaign is one to ensure the continued existence of the human race. That is the goal. *And I have said over and over again, although I do not seem to be noticed when I say it, that it is not enough to ban nuclear weapons. If you ban nuclear weapons completely, and even destroy all the existing stocks, they will be manufactured again if war breaks out. The thing you have to do is to ban war,* and the problem is, how are you to get the peoples of the world into a mood in which they can really ban war? I think that this is a first move which might do something towards making the nations a little less unwilling to take the steps that are necessary. *(Our italics)*

But even Bertrand Russell is not yet clear as to what he believes and we attribute this much less to the passing of the years than to "contamination" by politicians. He regards the Motion as "a first move" in a long campaign. The Motion proposed by Lord Simon was

> "to persuade HM Government to take definite action, first, to stop the spread of nuclear weapons to other countries by ourselves offering to forego, and abandon the use of, such weapons: and secondly to persuade the United States of America and Russia to help the United Nations to control and enforce the necessary treaties."

It would seem, from the foregoing, that there are two problems: a short-term one: to persuade the government to stop the spread of nuclear weapons; and the long-term problem of "how to get the peoples of the world into a mood in which they can really ban war". To take the second "problem" first. Where *are* in fact the people who are in the mood to *wage* war? Whatever the psycho-analysts may say about aggression and its relationship to war, which country in the world is able to wage war — or for that matter maintain an army at "required strength" — without conscription or the economic pressure of mass-unemployment? In that case, when Russell talks of the "mood" in which the people can "really ban war" he means the mood in which they can *prevent the politicians from going to war in spite of their (the people's wishes)* . . . which is quite another matter. And if that is what he means now can he, at the same time, expect the Government to take the first step of stopping the spread of nuclear weapons? He was asking something which no self-respecting politician would undertake to do. And even the spokesman for the pensioned-off Labour politicians in the Lords, Viscount Alexander of Hillsborough thought

> it would be far wiser for my Party at any rate, to wait and see whether or not we are bound to go with the manufacture of the bomb. That is the real position of the Labour Party. We do not want to manufacture these weapons, but we should not be left in the situation of being the only one outside the club. We have to keep in mind the interests of our general peace, being, as the noble Earl the Leader of the House has described our country, the centre of a great Commonwealth. I wish I could be more favourable from the general point of view of the objectives of my noble friends with regard to the bomb. I very much welcome the way in which they have presented their case to the House, but I most inform them that, in all the circumstances, I could not possibly ask my colleagues to assent to the Motion.

Hopeless as it may be to pin one's hopes on the people that they may one day realise what it's all about and rise up, it is worse than useless to expect the politicians, each one of whom is consumed by his own vanity and political and social ambitions, as well as devoid of any imagination or humanity, to take the initiative of a move which will weaken his position in the nuclear "club". Of the two choices, we still believe that the people are more likely to save themselves from disasters than are the politicians.

But we were saying earlier that war, of which nuclear war is but one disastrous aspect — is itself but an effect, whereas the causes lie deep in our social system. In the late 19th century both socialists and anarchists were unanimous about the causes of war. The 1914-18 war changed the views of the socialists (as well as of a few "eminent" anarchists who, however, ended their days in the political wilderness, unlike their socialist counterparts who became post-war prime ministers) and the "responsibility" of office in subsequent years has made them almost self-conscious of the importance of force as the principle argument in international diplomacy and the basis of government. Now, for the new generation of "socialist" politicians *government*, not socialism, has become the ends. Their ambitions would matter little but for the fact that in playing their game they have poisoned the Labour movement, destroying its socialist content and substituting for it a vote-catching machine.

How are we to get the peoples of the world in the "mood" in which they can really ban war asks Bertrand Russell, and we think the answer is if more people become so conscious of the potentialities of life and living that they will resent "selling their labour" to a boss, will hate authority and the social system based on it. They then will resist war not because they are afraid to die but because they believe in life, and in a life-positive world there is no place for war, warmongers and politicians.

Propaganda we think must be directed into these channels. We agree with much that the Direct Action Group is doing but they do not go far enough. When they now call on people to withhold their votes from election candidates who are not prepared to support their demand for nuclear disarmament they are simply hoping to blackmail the candidates. What they should be doing instead is persuading the electors not to vote for *any politician*. Only when as individuals we refuse to have someone to act for us, will we begin to *find the time and learn how to act for ourselves*.

(February 21, 1959)

WHICH ROAD FROM ALDERMASTON?

Last year's march to Aldermaston was a simple, moving, demonstration to the people of this country and the world that some of us viewed human survival as more worthwhile than national pride. For by advocating unilateral nuclear disarmament for Britain they were in effect declaring that they were prepared to see this country excluded from the Executive of the Big Powers, and relegated to the ranks of the third-rate powers without a voice in the political "destinies" of the world. As a gesture, as an example for others to follow, the March was imaginative and positive.

Yesterday the marchers were again on the road. This year however they started in Aldermaston; their destination, London. For, in the words of the organisers

> Aldermaston, the source of the weapons we oppose, has become a symbol of our unity of purpose, but London is the centre of political power which controls Aldermaston. This year, then, we march from Aldermaston to London.*

If Aldermaston has become the symbol of "our unity of purpose" what will London, "the centre of political power" become? The symbol of disunity?

* *Campaign for Nuclear Disarmament Bulletin*, January, 1959.

If the March is not to become simply an annual airing for our consciences, a routine "must" for progressives, which will be deadly and ineffectual as are the official Labour May Day parades, then it is more important that this year's March should be the occasion for earnest discussion among the marchers themselves than a demonstration to fire the imagination and win the support of the bystanders who will be met *en route*.

Since last Easter, the "unity" of the Campaign has been disturbed by a small, active body of people calling themselves "The Direct Action Committee Against Nuclear War" whose first public action directed to the Missile base at North Pickenham last December was given front-page prominence in the National Press and caused the respectable and responsible Executive Committee of the Campaign for Nuclear Disarmament such acute embarrassment that they found it necessary to issue a statement disassociating themselves from the rebels. It is worthwhile reprinting the statement for at the same time it summarises the Campaign's own position.

> Supporters of nuclear disarmament have been widely criticised in the Press for abandoning the methods of persuasion and undertaking civil disobedience at the week-end demonstration at North Pickenham. I would, therefore, like to make the position of the Campaign clear.
>
> We aim to change public opinion and the policies of the political parties through the usual democratic channels. We work in friendly co-operation with a number of other organisations, including the Direct Action Committee against Nuclear War which was responsible for the demonstration at North Pickenham. It is an entirely independent organisation with which we have co-operated on many projects, including the Aldermaston March and Vigil.
>
> The National Campaign for Nuclear Disarmament is not in favour of civil disobedience or sabotage so long as reasonable opportunities continue to exist for bringing democratic pressure on Parliament. It recognises that those taking part in the North Pickenham project did so in full knowledge of the risk involved of violence or legal action. We also realise that many who support our aims have been encouraged to take part in such activities through the failure of a great deal of the National Press to report either fairly or adequately our legitimate activities.*

Spurred on by the success of their first venture, the Direct Action Committee (which is composed of pacifists, and whose vice-chairman, Hugh Brock, is editor of *Peace News*) has now launched a Voters' Veto campaign which aims at persuading people to vote only for candidates who declare that they will support the campaign for nuclear disarmament in the House of Commons irrespective of Party Whips and party policy. Where no candidate in a constituency is prepared to give this undertaking voters will abstain from voting altogether. North Pickenham was a youthful escapade

---

* *Campaign for Nuclear Disarmament Bulletin*, December, 1958.

which a disclaimer and the passing of time would help everybody to forget. But the Voters' Veto was really putting the cat among the political pigeons. On the brink of a general election these irresponsibles were launching a campaign which, if successful, would operate against the Labour vote and thereby assist the Tories into a third term of office.

Not only did the Campaign for Nuclear Disarmament issue a 4-page supplement to its February *Bulletin* reprinting the Direct Actionists' letter to the *New Statesman* and Ben Levy's reply which they stated "has the general support of the Executive Committee of the Campaign" but a number of "pacifist" and sympathetic MPs have expressed themselves, some of them more in anger than sorrow, in the columns of the *New Statesman* and *Peace News* on the dangers of the campaign for a voters' veto.

It is significant that the circular letter addressed to all MPs and prospective candidates of the three main parties asking them whether they supported the unilateral nuclear disarmament campaign by Britain and if so whether they would be prepared to vote against nuclear weapons in the House of Commons, "defying if necessary the Party line", has brought only 86 replies. Of these only 34 (31 Labour and 3 Liberal) MPs *and candidates* said they supported the policy of unilateral disarmament but only 6 Labour and 1 Liberal *candidates* said they would be willing, if necessary, to defy the party whip. *Not one of the nine Labour MPs who replied in the affirmative to the first question would do likewise when it came to defying the party whip.* And these nine include household names among pacifists such as Frank Allaun, Fenner Brockway, Emrys Hughes, Victor Yates and Reginald Sorenson!

In their canvassing of electors in the S.W. Norfolk by-election they seem to have had more success, with 165 supporting Voters' Veto and a further 104 who support Nuclear Disarmament "considering withholding their votes" out of 1,186 people so far canvassed. But for Voters' Veto to be more than a symbol, the Direct Action Committee would need thousands of canvassers operating throughout the country simultaneously. And we believe that long before that situation was reached Voters' Veto would have become redundant.

Whilst it is not difficult for us to feel much sympathy for, and closer to, the workers in the Direct Action Committee than to the Campaign for Nuclear Disarmament, we must recognise — with regret — that basically both organisations have not only aims in common but rely on the same means for achieving them. However much the Campaign for Nuclear Disarmament disowns civil disobedience and decries the voters' veto campaign of the Direct Actionists both organisations look to Parliament to legislate for unilateral nuclear disarmament. The Campaign for Nuclear Disarmament talk of "changing . . . the policies of the political parties through the usual democratic channels" while the Direct Action Committee in the opening paragraph of its most recent statement on the "Political Implications of a Voters' Veto" declares

> The campaign against nuclear weapons is a rebellion against a national policy based on preparations for genocide . . . the H-Bomb is the supremely important moral issue of today. But this is a political as well as a moral issue. *Eventually it is a British Government acting in the name of the British people that will renounce the Bomb.* The rebellion has got to be taken directly into politics. (Our italics.)

Where the two organisations disagree is on the tactics to be adopted at this stage. The National Campaign for Nuclear Disarmament on the one hand

> is not in favour of civil disobedience or sabotage *so long as reasonable opportunities continue to exist for bringing democratic pressure to bear on Parliament* . . . (Our italics).

The Direct Action Committee, on the other hand, declare:

> Not only have we been disenfranchised to a large extent, but so also have our representatives in Parliament. Vital decisions are made in closed meetings . . . *In this situation the people must take action, and assert their right to have a voice in matters most vitally affecting them.* Where the constitution ceases to give them this right, the people are only exercising their democratic prerogative in taking non-violent action to exert pressure on the Government. (Our italics.)

It seems clear to us that, on paper at least, they disagree on tactics because they cannot agree as to how democratic or undemocratic are the Parliamentary- and Party-machines.

We think it not difficult to chart the course of the National Campaign for Nuclear Disarmament. So long as the money comes in it will proceed in a vicious circle of hope in Labour, and once Labour is in power (and Mr Bevan eloquently pleads for the H-Bomb as the most potent weapon for world peace in his armoury), the Campaign will be split from top to bottom and die from neglect.

Much more difficult to prophesy is the future of the Direct Action Committee, for its course is uncertain. North Pickenham was a carefully prepared and admirably executed demonstration which not only drew attention to the building of a missile base, but, more important, showed how precariously balanced is Authority with all its forces of law and order, and its armed forces. A mere handful of *determined* people refusing to play the game according to the rules could upset them all from the Home Secretary to the magistrates, from Chief Constables to ordinary coppers. Imagine the effect of a hundred North Pickenhams every week, requiring fewer people than will be marching from Aldermaston this week-end!

Whatever may have been the motives of the organisers of the North Pickenham demonstration, its impact was a moral, a-political one. It made people aware of the power that is in each of us *if we choose to use it*. And because the demonstrators were ordinary human beings, some with families (and all that is implied in the way of "responsibilities") who were prepared to spend a public holiday in prison, their action could not but give strength to others by example. This to our mind is the seed of rebellion not just against nuclear weapons, but against authority, of which Parliament is the living symbol.

For this reason it is difficult to find a connecting link between North Pickenham and Voters' Veto. One can only suggest that the success at the missile base went to our friends' heads. For the first action depended on the determination of those who took part, whereas the second requires a huge political machine and a millionaire's Press if it is even to dent the Establishment. The first is within the compass of any determined human being; the second smells a bit of political vanity and ambition. And if Voters' Veto is in fact a political campaign then it is doomed to failure (surely, the response to the Direct Action Committee's circular letter to MPs and candidates should convince them of that?) . . . and the Direct Action Committee with it.

We imagine that only a few of those of us taking part in the Aldermaston March have any illusions as to the influence such a demonstration will have on British "Defence" policy. On the other hand, we are not suggesting that since it has no effect on the government it is a waste of energy. There are times when the importance of an action is for onself. For some the very fact of having broken away from the routine pattern of life to take part in this March; for others the effort of will needed to join in a demonstration for the first time in their lives, are all positive steps in the direction of "rebellion" against the Establishment. But for the rest of us, as we suggested at the outset, this March though in the opposite direction is along the same road as last year: the A4 for the motorist, the reformist road for the majority of progressives. Last year it got us nowhere, and unless our thinking follows other roads it will get us nowhere this year.

The prospect of abolishing nuclear weapons in a foreseeable

future is remote indeed, even assuming that one persuaded the Government of this country to disarm unilaterally. The threat of fall-out from tests, or annihilation as a result of nuclear war between Russia and the United States remain. Even assuming that all countries agreed to nuclear disarmament, that is no guarantee, for as Bertrand Russell pointed out in the House of Lords debate on the subject last month: "it is not enough to ban nuclear weapons. If you ban nuclear weapons completely, and even destroy all the existing stocks, they will be manufactured again if war breaks out. The thing you have to do is to ban war". And to this end "we must work towards some system which will prevent war. It requires a different imagination, a different outlook and a different way of viewing all the affairs of men from any that has been in the world before".

That "different outlook and imagination" we submit must come from the people and not from governments. If we recognise (and in our view there is ample evidence to prove it) that the existing economic system creates and perpetuates social injustice as well as slumps and unemployment, which only a war or a war economy alleviate; that the centralisation of power creates strife within the nation and between nations, and that in the struggle for power, war is a potent argument — then the only practical action is that which attempts to remove these *causes of war*. To seek solutions through the existing organisms of society is not only unrealistic, but downright silly.

There are no short-cuts to peace. There are no compromise solutions between the rulers and the ruled. The day when we will be in a position to influence governments we shall also have the strength to dispense with governments. Until we can put short term prospects in their proper perspective we shall continue to overlook the long term aims which alone can ensure a world at peace. For the past twelve years we have been engaged on the problem of imminent annihilation by the Bomb or enslavement by the other side. After twelve years we are still where we were, and in spite of all the wise men "guiding" our political destinies we are still living with annihilation or enslavement on our doorstep. Are we not yet satisfied that these methods of solving mankind's problems get us nowhere?

Is it not time people stopped worrying about the imminence of annihilation, for it's obvious that we are not able to do anything about it, if the politicians decide to press the button? If only a fraction of the energy now used in trying to reform our delinquent system were devoted to developing what Bertrand Russell calls a "different imagination", we have no doubt that in another twelve years' time we would be able to point to some progress on the solid road to peace.

This is our message to fellow-marchers on the A4!

(March 28, 1959)

HOW WOULD WE BAN THE BOMB?

It was during the frequent stops that one of our marching companions, who had read his copy of FREEDOM, put the question: "If this demonstration gets one nowhere — so far as banning the bomb is concerned — what kind of action do you think *would*?" We could not think of an answer which would not contain a hundred qualifying "ifs" and "buts". Here we were, 15,000 people walking from the Albert Hall to Trafalgar Square being handled by the police as if we were a procession of motor cars among motor cars, stopping at crossings to let the traffic through and taking our turn with the columns of buses in Whitehall. Two hours after the leaders had entered Trafalgar Square columns of marchers were still inching their way up Whitehall.

Compare this with the occasions when the Queen sets off for King's Cross Station. Then police are posted at every road junction and traffic lights are switched off to ensure that her car will nowhere be held up. Or when she attends some piece of pageantry or an official dinner, the roads in central London are closed to traffic, and special notice boards are posted up all round the prohibited area and the traffic is left to manage as best it can.

It must surely have been obvious to some of the 15,000 marchers that if no special arrangements could be made by the authorities to facilitate *their* march through London it was also very unlikely that the Government would bother to pay much attention to the demands over which some 3,000 of them had marched the 53 miles from Aldermaston. The Campaign for Nuclear Disarmament declares that it aims "to change public opinion and the policies of the political parties through the usual democratic channels". This presupposes that we live in a democracy, but if 15,000 citizens do not equal one VIP it is obvious that we still have a long way to go along the road to democracy.[1]

It is also clear, however, that in a democracy the wishes of 15,000 people, however sincere and determined they may be, at most represent only an important minority of public opinion. It may be frustrating to feel that probably a majority have no opinion of their own, but can one by-pass that problem without supporting authoritarian ideas and methods which invariably perpetuate the existing machinery of State, government and privilege? Free elections, the so-called "usual democratic channels" dear to the hearts of our political reformists are a Hobson's choice; one is free to choose among a number of aspirants to positions of power, but never to question the machine of government which they operate; one is free not to vote but not free to ignore the decisions made by governments which apply to every man, woman and child whether they voted for or against or not at all.

It is not without significance that *anarchy*, "absence of government", is also defined as "disorder, confusion" not only by the *Oxford Dictionary* but by most "progressively minded" people as well. Anarchy, they argue, is possible only in sparsely populated rural communities in an age of the hand loom and the individual craftsman, where time and science stand still and ambition is dormant. Modern society, with its dense agglomeration of urban population, its mass production and mass needs cannot afford the luxury of anarchy. (If only one could detect a little anarchy in their small family groups, one might be convinced of their objectivity.)

We anarchists remain unconvinced by this argument because we see that whilst mass production can lead to the creation of Mass Man, it is also the key to a society of leisure in which man can be himself, *because* freed from a preoccupation with sheer physical survival. We are anarchists because we believe that life is bread not as an end but as a means to an end. And we believe in the possible achievement of anarchy because we are convinced that more than ever before in man's history, we have a choice: between using our knowledge for our own destruction or for our emergence as human beings; between Mass Man and Individual Man.

1. As we go to Press we have read a report of the speech made by Mr Bob Willis, chairman of the TUC, who declared that "he was astonished and dismayed to see that the authorities had not stopped the traffic for the marchers" and went on: "If we have to have demonstrations in the future the authorities should realise that a procession against mass suicide is as important as a procession with gilded carriages". Canon Collins then quickly said that the police, carrying out their instructions, had been extremely helpful. *(Manchester Guardian.')* Whose instructions? That, surely, is the important point. Presumably from the same authority which decides to close the streets to traffic when the gilded coaches pass through?

The sneers and the jeers, the compassionate smiles we received from the politically-bound, Party-Leader-saturated marchers as we offered them FREEDOM "The *Anarchist* Weekly" far from being discouraging, convinced us that the alternatives are not between party and party, but between centralisation and decentralisation, between centralised authority and individual responsibility. In other words a political de-intoxication; a growing contempt for political expediency born of a growing belief in individual responsibility.

How would we anarchists ban the bomb — that was the question we started with and which we have apparently studiously avoided answering so far though not *in fact*. For have we not made it clear that the H-Bomb — and what is much more important, *war* itself[2] will not be banned by attempts at persuading governments or by direct assaults on government itself? After all when Labour won an overwhelming majority in 1945 did they dispense with the machinery of force? And is there any evidence that government, whatever its political colouring, can reconcile such white-blackbirds as authority, privilege and Mass Man with freedom, justice and the individual?

The anarchist road is undoubtedly a slow one, but since one of the speakers at Trafalgar Square last Monday was talking about the demonstration *next* Easter, we must not feel that our road is any slower than that of the political optimists, the more so since we believe that our road leads somewhere. We think there are two kinds of necessary activity. On the one hand any kind of protest is salutary, if only for ourselves. As one of FREEDOM's editors, the late Marie Louise Berneri, once put it so simply:

> It may be true that our protests will not change the course of events, but we must voice them nevertheless. Workers all over the world who rallied to the defence of Sacco and Vanzetti were not able to save them from the electric chair, yet who can say that their protests were useless?[3]

But at the same time if the enemy to human emancipation is the State and government, and we are agreed that we cannot easily destroy them by direct assault, then the only alternative left to us is to eventually destroy them by attrition, by withdrawing power from them as a result of taking over direct responsibility for more and more activities which concern our daily lives. That governments are more aware of the dangers herein involved to their power and indispensability than are people of the possibilities of real freedom, if only they took the plunge, is shown by the political par-

2. See "Which Road from Aldermaston?"
3. *Neither East nor West*, Freedom Press.

ties' "social plans" on the one hand, and the despondency and apathy of the people on the other. Whatever credit the Labour Party may claim for improved working conditions and living standards in this country must be offset by the new aura with which they have surrounded State and Government.

In the past fortnight the Tories, in their pamphlet "The Responsible Society", have been at pains to show that they are human and understanding and anxious, in the words of the *Manchester Guardian*, to make "the worker's life more bearable". They even put forward the view, when dealing with the welfare state, that

> "security, even automatic or unearned, is not necessarily demoralising: it is as much a springboard for vigour and family devotion as insecurity — the whole history of the middle class is evidence of this".

And any time now we can expect Labour's Plans for Leisure which will include a State subsidised National Theatre Chain and State financial assistance to all kinds of sporting and cultural initiatives as well as the supplying of instructors and organisers to "go out and build up creative leisure activities".

We can well imagine that Labour's plan will be warmly welcomed by the "progressive" elements in the acting profession as well as by their counterparts on the other side of the footlights and cited as yet one more reason to vote Labour when the time comes. But cannot these people see that by allowing the political parties to take the initiative of organising even our cultural and leisure activities, and incorporating them in the responsibilities of government (even if they operate through an Arts Council and not through a Ministry of Culture) they are consolidating the power of the State and at the same time limiting our freedom of action both as individuals and as artists?

We are not saying that the idea of a National Theatre Chain rather than a National Theatre in London is not a good one. But why should its establishment be a matter for government, and government finance? Are there not enough people connected with the theatre, either as executants or as spectators, sufficiently interested in this art form to come together and launch a nation-wide appeal to raise the funds needed for such a project? After all when the Government takes the initiative it is only providing the money from the public's purse, by force, of course. It is perhaps simpler that way and guarantees jobs for a number of actors and a show for the public. But who would deny that what springs from the people's own initiative is always better or that what is sponsored by the State is almost invariably academic and unenterprising? And in addition to these arguments for individual and group initiatives is the one that the more we do ourselves the more we will want to, and know how to, do for ourselves.

We must starve the State of initiative. Every radical worthy of the name has shared Jefferson's view that "that government is best which governs least". Both the Labour and Tory Parties promise us *more and more government*. It is up to us to resist this threat by protest and demonstration (not so much for the Government's sake but to draw our fellow citizens' attention to the dangers) and through our actions, showing by our sense of community and initiative, that we are more than capable of running our own lives — including the enjoyment of our leisure hours.

What can we do to ban the H-bomb? Very little, friends, until we decide that running our own lives is an important part of life for which we will *always "find the time"*. When we "find" or "make" this time we shall have little time or patience for the antics of politicians and power maniacs, or, energy to waste on making weapons for our own annihilation!

(April 4, 1959)

REFLECTIONS ON CAPITALISM AND WAR

One of the "positive" by-products of war, and cold war, we are told, is a speeding-up of scientific research, in most fields, to the material benefit of mankind. One of the benefits of the capitalist economy is that competition for markets results in technological advance with a consequent expansion of production, which not only benefits the industrialists and shareholders, but brings within the financial possibilities of large numbers of families the "labour saving" gadgets and the means for "enjoying life to the full", such as motor-cars, TV sets and air-travel, which less than fifty years ago were luxuries which only the very rich could afford. It is also argued, and there is plenty of evidence to support the view, that money incentives do encourage people to work harder, to use their brains and skill to work more efficiently and effectively.

All these arguments, however, prove very little beyond the fact that scientific research is speeded up in time of war; that mass production in a capitalist economy requires mass markets for its survival; that money as well as being the "root of all evil" is also the open sesame to the satisfaction of the material luxuries which a growing number of people equate with the pursuit of happiness.

But all this does not prove that war is the *only* method of speeding up scientific research, or that capitalism is the *only* way to mass produce the goods and services mankind needs to maintain life and health, any more than money is the *only* incentive which induces people to work harder or more intelligently. Today the "good" things that emerge from the system are almost without exception accidental or incidental. They occur not because the welfare of mankind is the end in view but, as we said at the beginning, as by-products in the course of maintaining and furthering the health of the System. And the system, in more concrete terms, means the interests — the power and/or economically privileged status — of a small section of society.

(Those of our readers who squirm when we use these terms and mutter: "Nineteenth century clichés; the trouble with the anarchists is that they have not advanced beyond Kropotkin; times have changed", would be well advised to read the City Notes of their daily papers, or brood on last Sunday's *Observer* with it's "Brewery Table Talk" by Pendennis or Alan Day's "Ethics of the Take-Over" to realise that *plus ça change, plus c'est la même chose*. What is no longer the same, is that today no radical or revolutionary shares the optimism of his nineteenth century predecessors. A significant fact, for to our minds, it is a clear indication that the "system" is stronger, not weaker, than in Kropotkin's day, *though the material conditions of the "masses" — in the industrial nations — are incomparably better than they were then.)*

Who was it who said "War is the health of the State"? We think that today this simple truth needs to be reworded and expanded because the System is stronger, more complex and the power struggle more pathological than it was.

For the 19th century socialists and anarchists the basis of war was economic, not ideological. There were colonial wars, which were straightforward piracy, either between rival exploiters for sources of raw material, or wars of subjugation. Then there were the wars between the great powers which were an "inevitable" aspect of the capitalist system. Today colonialism by the old methods is financially unprofitable, as well as militarily untenable in the long run (Algeria, Kenya, Central Africa, the Belgian Congo and South Africa are examples of old style colonialism which are doomed to failure — a process which can be hastened if only we help the "natives" to help themselves).

War between the Powers has also become untenable because, once launched, is uncontrollable. For this reason the industrialists, through the politicians, seek to resolve the ever-present "contradictions of capitalism" by a permament war economy (a much more profitable way of dealing with the problem than war which, nowadays, not only destroys the "enemy" but the vital "markets" as well). But if war has become untenable equally the power struggle would be reduced to an obvious farce if the political spokesmen relied on argument alone, without the backing of force "if necessary".

That there is "no honour among thieves" applies equally to capitalism and politicians. The capitalist class is united only in defending itself against the working class, but basically it is monopolistic, which means survival of the richest. Similarly with politicians. Even if they play the game according to the rules; even if on occasion they will agree to compromise (to give prestige to the game of diplomacy in the eyes of the people), basically it is a struggle between ambitious, power hungry, mentally sick, men, through which each of them desires to satisfy his lust for the limelight. Among such creatures there can be no honour, no certainty that they will not press the button which will launch mankind into disaster. Each *trades* on the hope that his opposite number will believe him capable of such an action even though personally he might never be prepared to go so far. But it is obvious that he will not be in a position to create this doubt if in fact there is no button to press! Hence Bevan's famous Brighton remark that to remove the H-Bomb from Britain's armoury was the same as sending her Foreign Minister "naked into the conference chamber". And speaking as a politician he was right.

Today the vast expenditure on armaments and research is made to (*a*) appease the industrialists and save the system (*b*) to maintain almost-full-employment (for a number of reasons, the least important of which is the belief that workers have a right to live) and (*c*) to keep themselves up-with-the-Eisenhowers and the Khruschevs.

De Gaulle has made it quite clear, for instance, that for France to be a Big Power she must possess her home-produced H-Bomb. Her possession of The Bomb does not *in fact* change the East-West power set-up. But from the point of view of *The Game*, the blackmail, France will have status the moment she can demonstrate to the other powers that she too has a button to press.

But though possession of a stock of H-Bombs is enough to ensure the destruction of mankind — oneself as well as the "enemy" — the Powers continue their researches on weapons of destruction as if those they already possess are not "ultimate" enough.

For instance, the *News Chronicle's* correspondent, Bruth Rothwell, reported recently on the "Think Factory", a "casual place beside the sea in sunny California" where:

physicists, engineers, philosophers and anthropologists sit around in open sports shirts — thinking.

The Rand Corporation, as it is more politely called, is a non-profit company with no shareholders and no dividends and no product — only ideas on the development of more effective ways to kill people.

The palm-shaded Santa Monica beach is only a stone's throw away. Yet the 800 Thinkers (141 of them Ph.Ds, pay rates from 5,000 to 25,000 dollars a year) are too busy thinking to relax.

Their world is at least five years ahead of the rest of us and when they dream, it is of ion rays and space ships far closer than the comic strips.

Rand — the name comes from Research and Development — was formed just after World War II by the U.S. Air Force to work, as the late General "Hap" Arnold put it in his founding memo, on "next-war research".

Only for politicians playing a game of make-believe is it possible to conceive of more "effective" ways to destroy mankind than are available at present.

So today instead of "war is the health of the State" we would say

"A War Economy is the health of Capitalism; cold war the basis of power politics. But war is universal death."

(June 6, 1959)

THE LABOUR PARTY'S DAMP SQUIB

It was very soon clear that the revised joint statement on nuclear weapons and disarmament issued last week by the Labour Party and the Trades Union Congress was no political bombshell, but a damp squib which will neither prevent the growth of the Nuclear Bomb Club, nor "unite" and strengthen the Labour movement in readiness for the electoral fray when it comes. For the leaders have committed themselves to nothing new.

They reiterate their determination to extend indefinitely the H-Bomb test suspension which has been observed by the three members of the Bomb Club since November. And because "it has now been accepted by the Medical Research Council that all exposure to radio-activity is potentially dangerous, and the greater the exposure the greater the danger (so) that there is no 'safe limit' " the Labour Party will continue to observe it even if "other countries were to break the truce". In such a case they would "immediately initiate fresh negotiations for an international ban on all tests".

They make it equally clear that there is no question of their accepting the policy of unilateral nuclear disarmament by this country — a policy which has been "decisively rejected both by the Trades Union Congress and the Labour Party" for "nothing has happened to weaken the arguments against it". So all that the Labour Party will do if returned to power is to take the initiative of offering to give up the Bomb (made in Britain) if all countries except Russia and the United States agree to renounce any ambitions or plans they might have to produce their own nuclear weapons. The Labour politicians consider such a step deserving of praise by the foreigner and justifying a feeling of smug virtue by the Britisher, for

> We do not deny that in taking the initiative in a project which, if successful, would leave Russia and America as the sole nuclear Powers we should be making some sacrifice in power and influence. It was because of these considerations that the Labour Government decided in 1946 to make our own atom bomb, and that the Labour party decided some years later to support the production by Britain of her hydrogen bomb. But we hold that, in the circumstances and under the conditions we have laid down, this sacrifice would be abundantly justified in order to prevent the spread of nuclear weapons to more and more countries throughout the world.

The frank admission, that Britain joined the Nuclear Club for reasons of "power and influence" and not as some people seemed to think at the time, for reasons of "defence" against Russian threats to our "independence and freedom", exposes the Labour

Party's plan as worthless because one-sided. Indeed, the Labour politicians recognise this when they admit that

> we can hardly deny these nations the right to follow our example. For all the arguments which prompted us to make our British nuclear weapons can be used with equal force and validity by the French or Chinese, for example, for producing their bombs.

Such sweet reasonableness and tolerance indicate not a change of heart but that the political leopard does not change its spots, and that when the Labour politicians talk of making "sacrifices" in power and influence *if* their proposals are accepted, it is a lie, which de Gaulle, Adanauer and the others can see through without even looking.

There is only one way out of the present threat to mankind, and that is a gesture directed to the hearts and imagination of the *people*, not to the politicians who cannot afford either. That gesture should consist in announcing to the world that Britain is disarming completely. We stress this fact of *complete disarmament* because the Labour Party envisages the possibility of this country, as part of NATO strategy, ending her production of nuclear arms and concentrating her defence effort "on the building up of conventional forces, leaving the responsibility for the production of nuclear weapons entirely to the United States". Such a gesture could only earn the contempt of the world's politicians because they would see it as being contrary to all the traditions of the political game. The Labour Party statement confirms this view.

> There is not the slightest evidence that, if we were to take this step, it would induce America or Russia to follow suit or in any way influence the policy of General de Gaulle or the Chinese Government.

And they are quite right, but only because they think in terms of power politics and not of solutions which make their appeal to the people themselves.

And here we reach the impasse, the limitations of political parties. There is in fact no solution to the present arms race, nor to the specific issue of nuclear weapons, within the framework of power politics. It is a Gordian knot which can be cut through by revolutionary, unconventional methods, but will resist those who, even with the best intentions — and we do not include the politicians among them — would seek to unravel it.

What we are trying to say is this: if tomorrow the social conscience in this country could express itself, it would be useless to seek to use it to influence either the American or Russian Administrations. But, to our minds, it would have a profound influence if we directed that social conscience to the ordinary peoples of the world.

Can *you* visualise the persuasiveness of our arguments if we used only a part of the resources and human ingenuity now wasted in developing weapons of annihilation, for broadcasting to the world that we had abandoned them, and with the rest made a significant contribution to raising the standards of living of the starving other half of mankind? And are *you* aware of the fact that this could be achieved without lowering the existing standards of living in this country? Indeed, we could even "afford" to provide a decent living for *everybody* in Britain as well.

"That is all very fine, but it's not practical" — do we hear somebody object? "Not Practical" for whom? If you are thinking of the interests of the politician and the Trusts, we agree. Without the backing of force, deprived of privilege, they are lost; they are humble citizens like you and me. For *us*, the ordinary people, what we have proposed *is* practical because it is what we want. The Russian people want leisure, the necessities of life and they want to live in peace just as much as we do in this country.

But only by by-passing the politicians — whatever their professed ideology — can we acquire the power and the social responsibility as individuals which we need to build a world at peace; a world in which every human being will feel able to be himself.

(July 4, 1959)

DISARMAMENT?

In Washington last week Mr Khrushchev told the National Press Club that "it would be sheer madness to allow a new world war to come to a head". He was convinced that the Americans, like the Russians, were for peace. The following day at a luncheon in his honour he concluded:

> Having made your acquaintance, I am convinced you do not want war neither with our country nor with any other country of the world. Let us have eternal peace.

The same day, at his morning Press conference President Eisenhower commented on Mr K's National Press Club speech saying that

> he found the Soviet Prime Minister's manner and deportment extremely friendly, and he was convinced that Mr Khruschchev shared his horror of atomic war, which could result only in "the futility of mutual suicide". That was the one point on which they were in full agreement, but even there was the possibility of disagreement on specific issues of policy.

We would be among the first to warn against accepting that politicians meant, or believed the things they said, but the foregoing statements are in rather a different category, for the Big Two political leaders in this case are not whitewashing themselves *but each other!*

For years we have been told that the cold war was necessary to hold in check the aggressive ambitions of the Russians, or the Americans — depending from which side of the iron curtain the situation was being viewed, yet now Mr K tells the world that he does not believe that the United States have aggressive intentions against any country, and Mr Ike is convinced that Mr K shares his "horror of atomic war which could lead . . . etc." Assuming that both men believed what they said to be true, what prompted them to say these things? If they did not believe them to be true it is difficult to imagine what political or tactical advantage each could derive from whitewashing his potential "enemy".

In his opening statement in the general debate on Disarmament at the United Nations Mr Selwyn Lloyd for Britain put forward his country's plan for total disarmament by stages, a programme that would "rule out the possibility of aggressive war". Mr K also addressed the Assembly with a speech that hit the headlines, calling for a four-year programme to abolish all armed forces except of course "police units" for internal control.

> This meant that land armies, navies and air forces should cease to exist, that

general staffs and war ministries should be abolished, that military educational establishments be closed, dozens of millions of men return to peaceful creative labour.

Foreign military bases should be abolished. All nuclear bombs should be destroyed and their further production prohibited, their energy to be used for peaceful purposes.

Mr Herter for the United States said that the disarmament problem was one "deserving of all our imagination and ingenuity". There would be a growing danger in an indefinite continuation of the arms race which must be prevented from "exploding into nuclear conflict".

Mr K's disarmament plan which, except for the four-year limit, has (so we are told in last Sunday's *Observer*) a no more sweeping aim than the British plan, has apparently been received by Western Governments with "disappointment". And some UN delegates have written it off as "Utopian".

The main stumbling block to the Russian plan appears to be the question of inspection and control. Are these objections a reflection of the genuine concern of the Western powers to make sure that Russia carries out any agreement that may be reached on disarmament, or are they put forward as an excuse for continuing the arms race — possibly for reasons other than military ones? That the political observers are not so sure as to the answer is clear from a recent *Guardian* editorial (21/9/59) in which it is conceded that "Mr Khrushchev may be genuinely convinced that the West has argued about controls so as to avoid steps towards disarmament".

On the other hand it can be equally argued that if Mr K is "convinced" about the pacific intentions of the United States, and is anxious to strengthen the Russian economy by diverting the war economy to raising the standard of living in Russia and the underdeveloped countries of the world, then nothing is stopping him from taking the necessary steps independently of any agreement with the Western powers. Equally while it may be true that any agreement on inspection would provide the West with more new information about the East than the latter would learn of the West, what does it matter if Russia's intention is in any case to disarm completely? At present, however, it would appear that Russia's plan for complete disarmament allows an inspection system to operate only when it is no longer needed.

But whilst the political spokesmen of the West are urging that Russia should give proof of her sincerity over disarmament, what steps have been taken by the West to convince Russia of their own sincerity in this matter? According to Max Freedman in the *Guardian* (21/9/59):

almost everyone seems determined to ridicule Premier Khrushchev's disarmament proposals except President Eisenhower and Mr Herter . . . In private talks with reporters American officials have expressed the utmost scepticism about Mr Khrushchev's proposals to the United Nations, but they have refrained from public criticism.

No such restraint has been visible in the American press, whose attitude has ranged from mocking derision to contemptuous rejection. It has chosen to magnify every little episode of temper by Mr Khrushchev, every gesture that can convey the rough bluster and menace incarnate in this imperious dictator. Can such a man, the press asks with triumphant sarcasm, really be judged as a sincere friend of peace when he comes before the United Nations and asks for universal disarmament?

And what steps have the Americans taken to remove the anomaly of China's exclusion from the UN? Mr K was obviously right when he declared that "it was inconceivable that anyone could seriously think that a stable and reliable solution of major problems could be achieved without China". After all what would be the point of the West reaching agreement over inspection and control with Russia if a similar agreement with China were not made?

It is possible that Russia does want some measure of disarmament not because her rulers are peace lovers, but as Mr Philip Noel Baker, who met Khrushchev last December, put it in an election speech last week, for "the most practical and materialistic reasons; that his (Mr K's) plans for Russian economic progress will be gravely imperilled if the arms race goes on". The best test of Mr K's sincerity would therefore be to analyse the economic structure and situation as it is at present in Russia and decide whether there are grounds for accepting this theory. (It is interesting to note that Mr Herter is said "not to regard it as totally impossible that the Russian government may now be ready to accept a measure of genuine disarmament.)

Whereas no one seems to deny that the Russian economy could be expanded considerably without any problems of finding markets to absorb the goods produced, how to dispose of the almost limitless productive potential of American industry *is* a problem of the first order; so much so that for some considerable time American heavy industry has not been working to full capacity. And though Defence spending has continued to increase, and the standard of living in America is still the highest in the world, some four million American workers are without jobs. Is it reasonable to believe that the ending of the cold war and general disarmament would strengthen the American economy? Whatever may be the intentions of the American political leaders in this question of disarmament, there is no doubt in our minds that the industrialists and the real rulers of America will not hear of any plan which for them will only mean a further cut-back in production. Their obstinacy over China is no less significant than the concerted efforts of the American capitalist press to forestall any attempts at easing the so-called "tension" between the two power blocs.

America, in fact, cannot afford to end the cold war. But if Russia *can* then she has in her hand a trump card more far-reaching than any rocket, more (politically) explosive than all her H-Bombs put together. For by accepting all the conditions of control and inspection which the Western powers are demanding, and proceeding with her own disarmament, unilaterally if need be, not only would Russia be strengthening her economy but at the same time removing the excuse for continuing a cold war economy in the United States. Big business would of course soon find another enemy to threaten the American way of life and her "free-institootions" but there is no guarantee that the public would swallow the bait quite as easily this time. Or would they?

(September 26, 1959)

WHO'S BLUFFING?

Just as many political observers are of the opinion that the Macmillan Mission to Moscow and the subsequent Eisenhower Mission to Macmillan — at least in their timing — were calculated to enhance the Tories' chances at the General Election, so is it reasonable to suppose that Khrushchev's recent speech, which Michael Foot describes in *Tribune* as "full of hope and conciliation", may well be motivated by reasons quite alien to the cause of peace.

Similarly, Eisenhower's willingness, and de Gaulle's reluctance, to have an early Summit meeting should not tempt us into describing the former as a peace lover or the latter as a warmonger. After all, if at present Mr Khrushchev poses as a man of peace and the champion of complete disarmament, one can only assume that he does so because he believes that such a policy at this stage is more effective, so far as his government's political objectives are concerned, than the threatening, sabre-waving speeches he has also been known to make on other occasions.

Perhaps his disarmament "line" at the moment when Russian "achievement" in outer-space has captured the world's imagination (and we suggest that the world is more impressed with Russia's missile development than with her exclusive photographs of the Moon's backside), has been put forward in the knowledge that the Summit talks will come to nothing, but also in the belief that from the point of view of propaganda, of undermining the West and its satellites, of impressing the uncommitted peoples and the struggling colonial nations, such a line can do nothing but good . . . for Russia. And in the game of power politics one cannot altogether discount the value of this kind of propaganda particularly among the peoples of the "under-developed" nations who, one sometimes tends to forget in viewing the political game with the bleary eyes of the well-fed Western nations, represent more than half the world's people and are desperately hungry as well as desperate.

Obviously the Western powers cannot afford to ignore Mr K's proposals. If he is bluffing then they must call his bluff but they can only do this effectively by accepting the challenge and demonstrating that they are willing to take the first steps. Khrushchev's proposals are all-embracing: total disarmament!

But for those who accuse the Soviet Union of taking up a position of all or nothing, "that is, that we in proposing universal and total disarmament, are not willing to agree to anything else", the cunning Mr K points out that in his proposals it is written "in black and white" that should the Western powers "not be prepared to embark on universal and total disarmament, we regard it possible and necessary to reach agreement even on partial steps in the sphere of disarmament". And he then gave a general outline of Soviet policy on the subject:

> The Soviet Union is of the opinion that such steps include the banning of nuclear weapons, and, first of all, the termination of their tests, the creation of a zone of control and inspection, the reduction of foreign forces on the territories of relevant European countries, the creation of an atom-less zone in Central Europe, the liquidation of foreign military bases on foreign territory, the conclusion of a non-aggression pact between the NATO member states, and the member states of the Warsaw Treaty.

Those who argue that by scrapping the "ultimate deterrent" — the H-Bomb — Russia would have the advantage of larger conventional forces, should first propose abolishing conventional weapons and armies. In his present mood we are sure Mr K would agree! The only trouble is, that the three Western powers cannot agree among themselves.

France is busy using her conventional weapons in Algeria (half a million men and the latest in conventional weapons of destruction) and is also on the point of testing her first atom bomb which de Gaulle (like Bevan two years earlier), considers a weighty argument at any Summit meeting that may be arranged. Britain, according to last Monday's *News Chronicle* is now engaged, in the person of the new Defence Minister, in working out

> far reaching plans to rebuild Britain's dwindling forces to defend the country against conventional attack. They are first priority in view of the forthcoming Summit meeting.
> If the big Powers agree to ban nuclear weapons, Mr Watkinson will be faced with a defence reorganisation even more sweeping than the one carried out by his predecessor, Mr Duncan Sandys.
> A big increase in Fighter Command — both fighters and anti-aircraft missiles — will be the most urgent need.
> Other probable changes are:
> 1. A bigger Coastal Command to fight the submarine menace;
> 2. A rethinking of the Navy's role;
> 3. An increase in the standing Army above the present target of 170,000, with a possible return to conscription.

In the United States the disarmament question has, according to Max Freedman in the *Guardian* (9/11/59), "begun to divide both political parties". Eisenhower is still seeking an agreement with Russia "but reserves the right to have the United States resume underground tests of nuclear weapons if no adequate treaty can be negotiated with the Soviet Union. Mr Nixon supports this position without qualification". Governor Rockefeller, who hopes to be chosen for the Presidential nominations, has declared publicly that underground testing should continue in order to maintain "adequate defensive strength for American forces". And it appears that among the Democrats the division is even more acute. Senator John Kennedy, another candidate for the Presidential nomination, has challenged Rockefeller's position and come out for the continued suspension of tests, but former President Truman not only declares, in a newspaper article this week, that the U.S. should "immediately end its self-imposed ban on underground tests" but considers France's desire to become a nuclear power "all to the good". Mr Dean Acheson continues to be opposed to disarmament negotiations with Russia.

Mr George Kennan, former chairman of the policy planning staff under Mr Acheson, has once again, writes Mr Freedman, become the spokesman

for a large and important group in the Democratic party that chafes at the rigid approach of Mr Truman and Mr Acheson. Mr Kennan has proposed that the United States should take the lead in trying to eliminate nuclear weapons of all sorts. He believes that the present American policy of basing the security of this country primarily on nuclear weapons has failed.

Among the points made by Mr Kennan is that

under the sway of its preoccupations with nuclear weapons the United States has "grievously neglected" its conventional forces and allowed them to fall into a state where, in the absence of nuclear weapons, they would be inadequate to protect the nation's security.

Even the more "enlightened" members of the Establishment it would seem cannot think in terms of total disarmament, or even disarmament for that matter. The Kennan group are primarily interested in nuclear disarmament because the H-Bomb is not the deterrent it was made out to be, and he and his friends don't cherish the idea of more countries possessing nuclear wepaons. It is clear that only by abolishing these weapons will the small powers be put in their place and the proper balance of power re-established with conventional weapons. There is no talk of dispensing with force in the language of Western diplomacy. That old hypocrite Khrushchev however did have something to say about power politics:

There are statesmen in the Western countries who do not wish to give up their old views, alleging it is essential to have strength and to dictate to the weak from a position of strength . . .

but we will believe he is different when he starts practising what he preaches with his own people and those in the satellite countries.

The chances of a genuine disarmament are remote. Firstly because all governments rely on force, or the threat of force as the basis of their authority. Secondly because so long as nation states exist and the capitalist system of production and distribution persists, the struggle between nation states for markets, sources of raw materials, social and material privileges will be at the root of international strife. Thirdly because divide and rule is still the technique of power politics it was in the past. The Communist bogey is as much a factor in the emasculation of political and social thinking and progress in the West as the bogey of capitalism which serves to hold back the Russian people from rising against their oppressors. The Communist bogey has been an invaluable asset to the ruling classes of America, the Christian Democrats of Italy and de Gaulle in France just as the Capitalist bogey is fundamental to the continued "Communist" dictatorships in Russia and the satellites (Tito relies on both bogies!). Fourthly because in power politics the balance of power is always changing. We may yet live to see the day when America, Russia and Japan join forces to protect civilisation from the Chinese menace. Nothing should surprise us. Isn't de Gaulle after all biting the hand that fed him during the last war and shaking the hand that intended to ring his neck at the time?

There is no honour among thieves or politicians. Yet without honour in our relations there can be no peace.

(November 14, 1959)

CARPET BAGGERS ON THE MOVE!

The hotting up of "diplomatic" activity, the "goodwill" missions with leading politicians and heads of State queuing up to present their compliments, and their assurance of undying friendship, respect and admiration to the Queen, President or Chancellor, the forthcoming Eisenhower marathon (nine countries in two and a half weeks — is the President being "sponsored" by the Air Lines?) prior to the West's Big Four "pre-summit" meeting next month, are "a clear indication that . . ."., No, not that the world is at last on the brink of permament peace. If anything the comings and goings of these top-level carpet-baggers is a sign of a flare-up in the power struggle with the politicians jockeying for positions of advantage. As we were pointing out in these columns last week (*Who's Bluffing?*), the chances of a genuine disarmament were remote because, among other reasons, in power politics "the balance of power is always changing".

The idea that the world could be divided into two power blocs, the one dominated by Russia the other by the United States, and some "experts" even suggested that only thus could peace (albeit an armed peace) be preserved, overlooked the pride and experience of the grizzly professionals of politics with which Europe abounds, the messianic feelings of "dedicated" politicos, or the ambitions of a new generation of leaders (Paris- London- or Moscow-trained) apart from the powerful industrial trusts whose allegiance is to their balance sheets more than to power blocs!

What we are witnessing in the political field are attempts at breaking up the political and economic stranglehold exerted over the world by the United States and Russia. This process was started by Britain under Churchill in 1955 with the announcement in February of that year that Britain was building her own H-Bomb. It was clear even from Churchill's tactful remarks in a debate on the Defence programme that Britain's action was motivated by political and not military considerations.

However, Britain's failure to create a third Power Bloc was not really surprising. Apart from the fact that the politicians of Western Europe distrusted Britain's politics even more than America's, at least by tagging on to the latter she could be blackmailed into giving financial aid. With Britain they would get neither the aid nor the Bomb. But this did not mean that either France or Western Germany thought in terms of permanent subservience to the United States as part of the permanent division of the world into two power blocs. They, like Britain, also dreamed of a third bloc, in which they would play the dominant role. Without wishing to minimise the importance of de Gaulle in the present trend of European politics, any more than we would discount Hitler in the rise of Nazism in Germany, if today the Paris-Bonn Axis represents a threat to the political hegemony of Washington and Moscow it is not in the personalities of de Gaulle and Adenauer that one must seek the origins. It is a combination of political and economic actions and developments which have led to the present situation, and perhaps first and foremost was that of Jean Monnet, years ago when he put forward the idea of a European pool for coal and steel, and out of which has grown the six-country Common Market (France, Western Germany, Italy and the Benelux countries). The fantastic "economic" recovery of Western Germany is only in part the result of the acceptance of austerity conditions by the German people coupled with their "industrial genius". It is also the result of having lost the war. By not being allowed to rearm since, Germany has been able to concentrate on rebuilding her industries and cashing in on a seller's market.

But without military might as well Western Germany could not expect to play a leading role in world politics. And since it was unlikely that the occupying powers would be agreeable to giving her more than limited powers to rearm, de Gaulle was not only the Man of Providence for France but Adenauer's man as well. With Sahara oil on the horizon, Algeria is to de Gaulle and metropolitan France a liability, not an asset, and so far as he is concerned to have his armed forces freed from commitments in Algeria and a few atomic explosions to his credit, plus the economic marriage of convenience of the Common Market (whose steel production of 60 million tons compares very favourably with America's 77 million and exceeds Russia's 55 million), puts him in the running as leader of the Third World Force.

Writing before the official communiqués are issued, and not enjoying the confidence of the political leaders, we cannot speak with any authority as to the purpose of Adenauer's London visit this week. But according to one writer in the *New York Times*

In a moment of anger with the British early this year, Dr Adenauer told friends that Britain had to learn she could no longer lead the Continent, that France and West Germany were its leaders.

The same writer also points out that in the Franco-German vision of a third — a European — power that "might approach that of the Big Two", Britain would be excluded.

They feel that Britain seeks a special position as the "first among equals" among the allies of the United States and seeks, as she has always sought, to prevent the emerging of a dominant power on the Continent.

It would not surprise us, therefore, if the purpose of Adenauer's visit is simply to give Macmillan the sad news and perhaps to find out what counter-measures his old "friend" has up his sleeve. After all, Dr Adenauer thinks highly of Mr Macmillan, as witness his parting remarks to the *Guardian's* correspondent on the eve of his visit:

> His Conservative political philosophy is akin to my own, and I have learned to value him as an outstanding political personality.

All the more reason for distrusting him, surely, in the game of power politics.

But when at next year's Summit de Gaulle speaks in the name of "Frankenreich", as the Cologne *Rundschau* put it last week, Eisenhower and Macmillan will probably be more upset than Khrushchev, who to our minds is much less concerned by the East-West stalemate than with the longer term menace represented by communist China. Why should the Chinese leaders accept the permanence of Russian hegemony any more than Germany and France accept American domination? It is clear that, however inefficiently, China is making giant strides in the building up of its industries and war potential, coupled with a fanaticism once visible in Russia but which has since been replaced by a desire for the kind of animal comforts and tit-bits which are part and parcel of the American way of life. So Mr Khruschchev on the one hand is anxious to satisfy internal demands while on the other he anxiously watches developments in China. To have more or less apologised to India for China's armed provocations does surely indicate how concerned he is over his Eastern "ally".

One can view his New Look on the West as the stone to kill *three* birds. Fewer guns and uniforms; more refrigerators and saucy hats; more trade with the West and more financial "assistance" for the "poor" countries means more consumer goods for the Russian people and more allies for the Communist "cause". And this, the Russians probably hope, means alliances if and when China challenges their leadership, as well as undermining America and "Frankenreich".

When William Pitt the Younger, as Premier, was told by Napoleon's envoy that "the Emperor wants peace", he is reported as having replied: "No doubt, but what for?" The political approach has not much changed in more than 150 years, has it? No politician believes in peace for the sake of peace. So when Russia proposes disarmament the first question politicians everywhere ask themselves is "Why?" and tremble at the implications. Their suspicions are fully justified (but so are those of the Russians by any unexpected move from the outer side of the curtain). Three years ago when Russia announced that she was about to reduce her armed forces by 1,200,000 men Dr Adenauer declared that the announcement should be treated with "the greatest reserve" for no one knew whether the Russians were "changing their fundamental policies or simply their tactics". How right he was. But how obvious too. For no government ever changes its fundamental policies; which are, in the first place, to govern its own people; secondly to secure all the advantages it can for its ruling class internationally; thirdly to satisfy the vanity and ambitions of the professional politicians so engaged.

Governments only change their tactics, and it is just this that is currently causing such a pother in political circles. All the leaders from the highest to the lowest are on the move. Only de Gaulle can afford to stay at home — so long, that is, as one assumes Algeria to be still part of France.

(November 21, 1959)

1960

IS POWER POLITICS A HOAX?

One member of the serious Press, *The Guardian*, admits in an editorial on the subject of how much warning of a missile attack will be obtained from the radar chain now in course of construction, that

> only in a world gone slightly mad can there be serious argument about whether Britain would have four, five, ten or fifteen minutes warning of the surprise attack from Eastern Europe.

But being also one of the serious pillars of this "world gone slightly mad" the *Guardian* hastens to add:

> Yet the argument is serious, for on it depends whether the bombers and missiles based on Britain can be counted as a deterrent to major war.

And this of course is the official line put forward last week by the government's spokesman when discussing the Defence White Paper and explaining why, after all these years of goodwill missions, disarmament conferences and even the recognition last year, by Ike and Mr K that neither considered the other a warmonger, defence expenditure will be £116 millions more than for last year!

It is to our minds sheer lunacy to believe that a nation deciding to launch a missile attack on other nations will be deterred by such considerations as to the ability of the other nation to get enough H-bombs into the air before the missiles destroy them on the ground. None of the nations possessing nuclear weapons have any illusions about the boomerang effect of starting a missile war. Once started only wholesale extermination can be the outcome for mankind, and everybody knows it, and for this reason no one will knowingly start the conflagration.

What we have been experiencing since the end of World War II is unprecedented, and the result of the revolution in mass communications and in science and technology which was sparked off during the last war. We would suggest that power politics prior to 1939 was a much more real and potentially dangerous phenomenon of capitalist society than it is today. Then, whole continents were

Easter 1962.

I. Faces and Fashions

14 Easter 1962.

15 Easter 1961.

Easter 1961.

17 Easter 1960. Laurie Hislam (1909-1966). The lifelong protester.

...ary Canipa and Jack Robinson. Protesters in
... weathers.

Easter bonnet 1959 at the Albert Hall London last day.

21 April 29 1961 in Trafalgar Square before the Whitehall sit-down.

22 Easter 1959. Last day lunch break at the Albert Hall.

23 Sit Down February 7 1961 outside Defence Ministry.

the prize over which the colonial, the naval powers manoeuvred for advantages, for conquest. With the growth of nationalism and the liquidation of old-style colonialism (accelerated by the military needs of the colonial powers in their armed struggle against the military might of Germany and Japan), the power struggle between the nations has been modified radically.

That is, the *real* struggle, for it is an undeniable fact that however much frontiers may be modified, or countries "occupied" there can be no return to the approach of old-style colonialism. And this fact is all the more significant when one bears in mind that in terms of military weapons and techniques alone there is no reason why the colonial powers should not be in a better position now than they ever were to physically occupy and grind down the peoples of these territories.

It is equally significant that the military occupation of Western Germany has not prevented that country from rebuilding its industrial potential and raising the living standards of its people to among the highest in Europe. In world markets today Western Germany and not Russia is Britain's most serious competitor.

What then is the struggle for power all about? For many of us this is a question which has long ago been answered. To some of us it is simply the ambition of some nations for world domination; for others it is a question of economics, a struggle for markets in a world of shrinking markets. We believe that there are politicians whose lust for power is so great that they dream of world conquest. On the other hand we believe that in the world we live in there are so many ambitious politicians and industrialists as well as "uncooperative masses" to make the realisation of such personal dreams of world hegemony impossible. We are even coming to the conclusion that economic issues are no longer the dominating factor in the power struggle that they once were.

Indeed we are inclined to the view that the "power struggle" in international politics is a huge confidence trick in which so many people have a vested interest, that it is virtually impossible for any body of citizens to break the vicious circle. Apart from the "summit" leaders whose most pedestrian utterances are repeated by the Press and flashed on the TV screens in millions of homes throughout the world, every minor political leader has an interest in the maintenance of international "tensions" and of playing his role in the alignment of world power. But for it, Nkrumah could not dream of pan-Africanism nor Nasser of an Arab federation. And feeding the leaders are the hundreds of thousands of advisers, delegates and civil servants whose status and livelihood depend on the perpetuation of the power-political struggle. Again how would the thousands of political journalists earn their livings, as well as pontificate on TV and Radio, if there were no international political crises to unfold and to analyse?

Think of the number of career-men in the Services whose jobs and pensions would be affected if the Powers were to agree on disarmament. The Defence White Paper was a tonic to them. As the *Guardian* put it so tactlessly last week

> The Defence White Paper ought to please almost everyone ... The conventional forces are not, after all, to be cut further ...

Indeed, larger budgets are allocated to all three services, and by making the pay more attractive and pensions schemes more elastic the government looks forward to recruiting more ... allies!

Think also of all the technicians and scientists who depend on the power game for their well-paid jobs. The White Paper declares that 14 per cent of Defence Expenditure, that is £100 millions, will be spent on "research and development" this year. No wonder that the fate of mankind has now been reduced to a matter of minutes. After all, one cannot blame these scientists for taking a pride in their work!

What we have been trying to argue is that the "developed" nations — in science, technology and mass communications — are the victims of an *idée fixe* which has no bearing on reality. They have created an imaginary enemy, threatening at their doors, to justify the uncontrolled application of scientific knowledge to the development of lethal weapons and the techniques for their launching. These develop so fast that no sooner has production got under way than new discoveries make them obsolete.

How unreal is the whole armaments race, is surely shown by the recent announcement about the radar chain which the United States is establishing in this country and elsewhere at a cost of more than £100 million. For here we (or rather the Press) are worrying about the fact that we will only have four minutes warning of a surprise missile attack *when in fact it will take at least three years to build this detector which will give us four minutes warning of impending annihilation!* As realists we ask: "And what kind of an enemy are we facing who is proposing *to wait three years* to attack us when we know that he is able to land rockets on the moon now? Surely if one is dealing with a potential enemy who may at any moment launch a few nuclear missiles, one does not tell him where one's bomber force is located, nor inform him of one's armaments programme for the coming year. One certainly does not tell him that it will be years before one will possess a radar chain or that one's new tactic is to have mobile missile bases.

In fact one says nothing and acts. For is not attack the best form of defence? And if the West is only concerned with Defence and seeking to develop the finest instruments to this end, why don't we now give the enemy a taste of what he may give *us* in three years time when we have our detectors working our four minutes warning of impending annihilation?

If it's not all bluff, an expensive racket, why don't the "Democracies" bombard Russia with nuclear missiles *NOW!*

(February 27, 1960)

IS ALDERMASTON ENOUGH?

This week-end many thousands of people young and old will be once again on the road from Aldermaston to London. Their newsworthy actions will be duly recorded and noted by all the instruments of mass communications, while their protests will be studiously ignored by the government they seek to influence.

As a means for awakening interest in the threat to mankind by nuclear weapons, these marches may well be effective, although let us face it; even if twice as many people march this year as compared with last Easter, they still represent only an infinitessimal proportion of the country's population — or for that matter of the population along the route — and one wonders how many more years will pass before 100,000 people can be persuaded to give up even one day to express their solidarity with a cause which after all has the interests of everyone at heart. One cannot help noting that some six weeks ago more than 1,000 people set out on a 1,000 mile walk when the incentives were money prizes, and we have no doubt that next year Mr Butlin's money marathon will attract even larger numbers. We must not shirk such reflections for they make us aware both of the limitations of such protest movements as exist in this country today as well as of the problems which face all of us who would wish to make our contribution to the establishment of a world at peace.

The Campaign for Nuclear Disarmament rightly seeks to keep

party politics out of its demonstrations. Though we all know that the March will be largely composed of people of different political or religious denominations and allegiances, it is essentially a people's movement, of volunteers united by a common horror of the last word in scientific research, which threatens the future of mankind. But the CND ceases to be a non-political movement when it looks to political parties and governments to *implement* the demands put forward by the thousands of marchers and non-marchers who abhor the development of nuclear weapons.

In this respect the CND has suffered a set-back since last year's march, for it has always been the dream of the leaders of the movement that their plans would stand a greater chance of success if the Labour Party were returned to power. Hence the acrimonious debates with the Direct Action Committee over their Voters' Veto, which no democrat could challenge on *moral* grounds but which the CND attacked on the grounds that it would operate in favour of Conservative candidates at elections. In October last year the CND's hopes were dashed with the Labour Party's resounding defeat at the polls. For at least another four years they must face the fact that the government is a Conservative one which doesn't even take orders from its own Party let alone from an orderly column of Easter marchers. But also it is surely time that any remaining illusions they may have of Labour politicians were equally jettisoned in face of the Labour Party's recent performance over Defence Expenditure. The official Party line on nuclear weapons is no different from that of the government. The only considerations which would influence Labour Party policy are military, tactical and political ones, just as for the Conservatives, and 10,000 or 100,000 marchers offer no arguments which fit into this scheme of things.

To our minds the only effective function of an organisation such as the CND at the present stage is that of provoking more independent thinking among the people. This, as we, who are engaged in just such a task with FREEDOM, know only too well, is much more difficult than organising spectacular demonstrations which appeal to the emotional temperature of the moment, but which leave little trace once the organs of mass communications cool off and the provocative incident has been relegated to a paragraph in history and replaced by new provocations.

But of one thing we are certain, and it is that you will not induce people to think seriously and deeply, *through fear*. The CND, whatever the original motives of its founders, bases its public appeal on the fear of universal extermination in the event of an H-Bomb war. This is confirmed, we think, by the Campaign's refusal to be committed to a programme for total disarmament. Yet how can one effectively campaign for the abolition of nuclear weapons without provoking thought on, and eventually resistance to, *war itself* except of course by believing that one can build up a solid movement based on fear alone? Such a movement, however, will lose as many supporters as it gains, for most people can accustom themselves to fear, and live without it unduly upsetting their lives.

Let us face the fact that something more is needed if we are to build up a spontaneous movement of the people which will also be able to influence the course of events.

The Campaign for Nuclear Disarmament falls over backwards trying to be respectable, uncontroversial, and politically orthodox. Do we really have to spend time and energy campaigning that the results of war are horrible, and of H-Wars annihilation? This awareness of the disasters of war has not, so far, prevented wars.

What we have to succeed in getting across is that no thinking person will be a consenting party to any activity connected with war — under any circumstances. This is not just a question of persuading people to "sign a pledge" (how many of the million who signed such a pledge in the inter-war years ignored it when their call-up papers arrived?) but part of a new way of thinking and living which deals with the issue of war as part and parcel of a number of problems such as authority, corporal punishment, racial equality, freedom, religion, work, power, etc., . . . and not as something *exceptional*, outside the day to day problems of life. And this was the significant point in Bertrand Russell's statement: the abolition of war, he said, required "a different way of viewing *all* the affairs of men . . ." (note the word we have italicised). This is also the anarchist approach.

The CND in their publicity for this year's march call on you to "make this the Biggest Demonstration Britain has ever seen . . . In this way we might finally get rid of nuclear weapons".

These are all illusions. What have the government to fear from 100,000 demonstrators who politely express their anti-Bomb sentiments on four days of the year and behave as obedient sheep for the other 361?

(April 16, 1960)

THE CRAZY REALITY

All the parliamentary fuss over the Blue Streak Missile was simply the political game being played according to the rules, and will neither deter the government from pouring more money down the military drain, nor end the waste of human brains and materials on projects which are doomed to obsolescence long before they reach the stage of being mass produced. As Mr Watkinson put it when explaining away the £65 millions spent on the Blue Streak: "If we are to keep the peace for an occasional expenditure of £60 millions-odd, it is very cheap at the price". Apart from the fact that if it could be pointed out that such is the case, then the Opposition should be much more worried with the £1,500 million spent each year on "Defence", the Opposition surely is not in a position to criticise the Government's expenditure on the Blue Streak since its spokesman Mr George Brown was demanding a guarantee from the Government that

there will not be a period when there is no effective deterrent just because nothing will exist to carry it.

Thus the Labour Opposition has not offered an alternative to keeping up with the military Ivans — which involves the arms race we are now witnessing, but is at one with the Government in believing that this country should possess weapons which can be effectively directed against the enemy within the four-minute breathing space which the political and military leaders will be granted when the Fylingdales ear is operating in a few years time.

Now it is almost certain that by the time the Fylingdales project is completed the "enemy" will have developed a counter measure which will either neutralise it or, say, cut down the warning time to one minute. In which case all the bombers and what-have-you now being developed to make possible a massive attack within the four minute period will all be out of date, probably some time before the project is completed. As to what one should do in this case is a knotty problem for all concerned. You can only keep the enemy busy scrapping *his* latest weapons of "defence" and "attack" by rendering them obsolete as a result of the counter-measures *you* take to neutralise his latest weapons.

Supposing the West had not developed the H-Bomb, then it is probable that the East would not have developed it either. Once they both had it then each had to develop bigger and more efficient bombs and faster means of transport to carry them to their ultimate destination. Then the question was to devise a system of warning which would prevent you from being caught with your military pants down so as to convince the enemy that whatever he sent over you could return on the same scale. And we are now at this stage. Fixed launching bases are useless because the enemy can pin point them with his rocketry, so short of floating the British Isles and keeping the enemy guessing as to where we are from day to day, the Government has decided to try and keep our weapons on the move.

(What a lot of people seem to overlook, is that the very same problems that face the politico-militarists on this side of the power curtain are taxing their counterparts on the other side. For they too must provide the "deterrents" to nuclear attack from the West, since they no more believe the assurances of the Eisenhower-Macmillan faction than these believe in Khruschchev's doves of peace.)

Since the Labour Opposition is pledged to play this game it cannot, without leaving itself wide open to charges of hypocrisy and "political irresponsibility", object to the expenditure of huge sums of money on military projects which everyone knows will never be used. Think of the millions of young men who since the end of the war have been conscripted into the armed forces, housed, fed and clothed, trained in the use of weapons which have long ago been scrapped — all as part of a programme of "defence" or "deterrence". What greater waste of materials and man-power than that? Yet the Labour Government was responsible for this policy during the years it was in office and we can well imagine that its spokesmen could bring forward all kinds of arguments to justify the expenditure even though, in the event, not one of the post-war conscripts has fired a single shot against the "enemy" over the Curtain. Why then howl when the government decides to scrap a weapon when a mere £65 million (or £100 million — what is £35 million more or less in a millionaires' game? The answer is just one nuclear submarine!) has been spent on it. They should praise the Minister and his advisers for having come to a decision when so little had been spent on a weapon which the enemy had already neutralised. Thanks should also be voted for the enemy which had the decency to let us know in plenty of time that it was a waste of time to mess about with missiles launched from fixed bases!

But now of course in this country we are really up against it. *The Guardian* points to our dilemma in this "present insane race" when it declares

> The disturbing thing about the present thinking in the Ministry of Defence is that it does not seem to know what it wants to replace Blue Streak.

Government hopes however are based (perhaps this is not the

right word in the circumstances) on the use of missiles carrying bombers and possibly nuclear submarines. The latter are expensive toys (£100m each and according to a Pentagon spokesman 45 are needed for a "vengeance strike", that is about £1,200 millions for a set!) but very mobile, the former less expensive and less mobile, unless it is proposed to keep a striking force permanently in the air.

But enough of this crazy talk. It is crazy and real. And what makes these elaborate plans, these future projects, all the more crazy is the one real fact, which does not seem to be taken into account: that at any moment Russia and America, if they so wished, could blow the world sky-high, themselves included. And there they are, the politicians, scientists, and militarists, ponderously discussing "deterrents" in 1965, and four-minute warnings in 1963, and the Labour Opposition going through the motions of indignation about £65 millions and covering up their own moral impotence by taking it out of poor Black Rod, who had only come to call them away from their double-talk to the more rarified atmosphere of the House of Lords!

(April 23, 1960)

WAR OR CIVIL DISOBEDIENCE?

In a page-long article in last Sunday's *Observer*, Mr John Strachey, War Minister in the last Labour Government, attempts to analyse and demolish the arguments put forward by the various campaigners for British unilateral nuclear disarmament, presumably in order to justify the retention of these weapons by this country. It is of course not difficult to pick holes in their arguments. It is obvious that only multilateral disarmament, of conventional as well as nuclear weapons, will remove the threat of annihilation if a war between the major power blocs were to be launched. And if we have understood anything about the nature of government it is that it cannot function without force as its principal argument any more than the Christian Church could survive without "sinners". From a practical point of view then, the various approaches to the problem of unilateral nuclear disarmament, whatever else they may achieve, will certainly do very little to remove the threat of annihilation; and it was to remove this threat that an organisation such as the Campaign for Nuclear Disarmament was created.

But if Mr Strachey succeeds in pointing to the muddled thinking of the unilateral disarmers his own arguments are far from convincing or clear. In the opening sentence of his article he maintains that "full scale nuclear war is the worst threat to which the human race has ever been exposed".

Five columns later arguing that unilateral disarmament is in fact military surrender he opposes such a course for

> Surrender is surrender and it is merely pathetic to pretend that it is anything else. If the west, led by America (or conversely if the East, led by Russia) surrendered as wholes, that might well prevent nuclear war. But the price would be total submission — not merely military submission — to the will of the surviving alliance.

Surely Mr Strachey, whose whole approach to politics is that of choosing the lesser evil, should not hesitate to accept surrender and submission in return for the removal of the threat of nuclear war, for in his own words the latter *is* "the worst threat to which the human race has ever been exposed". If he means what he writes then nothing mankind could experience could be as horrible as full-scale nuclear war. Therefore he should argue that anything, any alternative, is preferable; even world domination by Russia or by America.

Mr Strachey supports the Labour Party's Statement, which proposes that Britain should abandon the independent deterrent while remaining a member of NATO; should depend on America for nuclear weapons while specialising in conventional weapons as her contribution to the Western alliance. He has come to see that there are important advantages in such a policy.

> They are not so much moral, as advantages in negotiating with other countries. For it may help to stop the spread of nuclear weapons and to confine their possession to Russia and America. I have always considered this as an important objective.

If the possession of nuclear weapons by two powers is to be preferred to their possession by one — for that, according to Mr Strachey, would mean "total submission" etc. — then why not encourage all countries to possess the nuclear deterrent? Are we to believe that Mr Strachey considers Russia and America more responsible than say Switzerland or Sweden? If so, then what's all this fuss about four-minute warnings and the latest American proposal for a permanent alert force in the air?

While agreeing with Mr Strachey that it would be an unhappy prospect for the world to have to bow the knee to Russia or America, which might, for a time at least, be the case if one of these powers were alone to possess the "ultimate" weapons of destruction, the prospect of a world divided into two camps dominated by Russia and America is hardly more inviting, especially when one considers that the price one pays for there being two masters in the world is the threat that nuclear warfare might be unleashed at any moment. But what Mr Strachey has at the back of his mind is reveled in the last paragraph of his article in which he declares that

> In my humble opinion the crux of the matter is that *one*, instead of two, or several, world authorities must sooner or later be established if we are to prevent nuclear war in the long run. There is not the slightest prospect of either of the alliances surrendering to the other and so giving us the other possible short cut to one world authority. But that the ultimate salvation of humanity lies in the evolution of such a single, unchallengeable world authority, I have come profoundly to believe.

It is significant that the writer spent some seven columns demolishing the arguments of the unilateral disarmers and only a short paragrpah to state that there is only one way out, and that it lies in the establishment of a world authority, "single, unchallengeable". This is all very fine, but how does he propose to go about it? To suggest that nations will renounce their sovereignty in favour of a world authority is no less "utopian" than the anarchist idea that human beings can live without authority from above. But its achievement is much less practical than that of an anarchist world, for whereas the anarchist appeal is directed to the oppressed of the world to shake off the parasites who feed on their labour and who seek to control every minute of their lives, the "world authoritarians" look to the politicians of all countries to abdicate their power and privileges to a supra-national body, just as if politicians were in the business for the good of mankind! We cannot repeat too often that the tensions, the crises, the misery and the strife in the world today are artificially created by a section of society for their own personal ends. They thrive on a divided mankind and it is therefore too much to expect that they should be willing to legislate for their own removal from the seats of power. World authority such as Mr Strachey seems to envisage it will only be possible when national frontiers will have ceased to exist and class barriers — social and economic — will have been abolished. And by that time the need for a world authority will no longer exist.

It would seem that at least a partial awareness of the arguments we have put forward above is penetrating some circles of the unilateral disarmament movement in this country. The "leakage" to the *Evening Standard* some ten days ago of the plan for a campaign of civil disobedience in this country, sponsored by Bertrand Russell and Michael Scott, revealed that some people within the CND have become aware of the futility of seeking to bring about radical changes through the so-called normal channels of Parliament. The "Committee of 100" for non-violent resistance to nuclear war can be considered revolutionary in the methods it proposes to adopt to "appeal to the conscience and intelligence of our fellow men". But the fact that it concerns itself with the problem of "nuclear war" only, leads one to assume that it will not allow itself to look upon the threat of war as part of the much bigger social problem. And we imagine too that the "Committee of 100" will limit itself to "warning mankind" of the dangers of nuclear war without encouraging "mankind" to dispense with the services of their politicians and take affairs into their own hands. We should be glad to be proved wrong. But certainly the idea of a large Committee with no office-holders, and the proposal that "no demonstration or other action will be undertaken without a minimum number of 2000 supporting volunteers", promise something more than token gestures of civil disobedience.

(October 8, 1960)

THE LP CONFERENCE AND NOW WHAT?

"It was painful today to follow the debate on defence in the knowledge that nothing said in the conference hall could substantially alter the result of the voting which had been settled before the debate began". Thus wrote Mr Francis Boyd, the *Guardian's* Political correspondent of the Labour Party conference at Scarborough last week. Mr Boyd must have a very painful occupation since such is the pattern not only of Labour Party conferences but of every parliamentary debate — with the exception of those very rare occasions when the Whips are called off and the vote is a "free" one. On those rare occasions it is said that the Member votes "according to his conscience". For the rest of the time he votes to the crack of the Parliamentary whip.

At Scarborough last week, on the day preceding the Defence debate, the question of the extent to which Conference decisions were binding on Labour MPs was argued at length, and for a very good reason. In view of the Executive's impending defeat on Defence, the National Agent reminded Conference of that passage in the constitution which says that "No proposal shall be included in the party programme unless it has been adopted by the party conference by a majority of not less than two-thirds of the votes recorded on a card vote". This it was clear the unilateralists could not achieve. On the other hand Conference carried, by 3,586,000 votes to 1,874,000, the motion that

> while acknowledging that the day to day tactics must be the job of the parliamentary party, declares that Labour policy is decided by the conference which is the final authority.

The National Agent, Mr Williams, insisted that the executive was only withholding its opposition to the motion on condition

> that every one understood that no change of policy was involved and that no one at all would have the power to "instruct, control or dictate" to the parliamentary party.

Mr Williams secured the rejection by 5,627,000 to 767,000 of a Nottingham resolution asserting such a power of instruction.

We confess to being unable to connect these two motions both of which were passed by a large majority. For if Labour policy is to be decided by the conference, which is defined as "the final authority" subject to the two-thirds majority clause, then presumably it *has* the power to "instruct, control or dictate" to the parliamentary party. If it has not the power then the Annual Conference is even more of a farce and a facade than one had already assumed it to be.

The argument put forward by the Parliamentary Labour Party to justify their independence from party control just does not stand up to examination. They argue that they are responsible to their constituents and not to the Constituency Parties, and least of all to a handful of Trades Union leaders who between them control several million votes at Conference. Now it is notorious that, on the major issues the Parliamentary Labour Party meet in private in the House of Commons and decide there what line they will adopt in the debate. And as we pointed out earlier, when the Division is called they vote according to the Party Whip. At no stage have their constituents been consulted on the subject of the debate or on the line that each individual MP should take in order to represent the views of his constituents. MPs in fact vote on the *Party* line every time. What valid objection can they have then to the Party, at Conference, determining the Party line for them? After all is it not the party which nominates them in the first place as its candidates, and supplies the funds and the workers to secure their acceptance by a majority of the electorate? The high-handed attitude of MPs to the Party conference when it seeks to control them is no different from the situation in the Trades Unions where the Union officials though ostensibly the representatives or the spokesmen of the members of the Union, act as if they were their Bosses. (An "unofficial" strike can only exist, surely, in an organisation where the tail wags the dog.) One MP in anticipating the defeat of the Executive warned the Conference that "it would be the first time in history that the conference has required the parliamentary party on an important subject to switch its policy between elections". The obvious way to avoid any undue embarrassment for such sensitive souls would be for the Party to hold its conferences once every four years or so, to coincide with an election spree. But then, we are assuming, or that MP was, that the Conference in fact instructs the Parliamentary party how to vote and to act.

In 1954 when the Party was once again meeting at Scarborough the burning question then was German rearmament and on that occasion the Executive, which supported the proposal, was saved by the skin of its teeth by the block vote of the Woodworkers who at the eleventh hour switched their vote — which only a fortnight earlier, at the TU congress, had been cast against the motion. The Labour correspondent of the then *Manchester Guardian* examining the prospects for the Party if the Executive were to be defeated on the German rearmament vote (for on paper it was inevitable; little did he know of the surprise that the Woodworkers held in store!) put it this way:

> If the rebels are successful and the official policy rejected then the brain reels at the conceivable consequences. Political logic would insist: the alternative is the abdication of the leaders whose policy has been overthrown or the acceptance by the leaders of a policy the direct opposite of their own. Either the party would be shorn of leaders (for their defeat would not be to the same extent a Bevanite triumph), or the leaders of their integrity (for if they bowed down before the will of the conference their new creed could only be an hypocrisy).
>
> The brain reels, logic insists. But at your shoulder the nagging critic is there to whisper, "Don't be a fool. If they're beaten, nothing at all will happen. No one will resign. There'll be a few fine speeches about Conference being the policy and the need to preserve the unity of the party and accept majority decisions. For a month or two Dalton or someone will be the spokesman, and the situation will change, and there'll be room once more for another Executive resolution . . ." An imp, too, propounds yet another possibility. There are to be two votes on Tuesday, so both resolutions could be carried in spite of one meaning precisely the opposite of the other. Everyone would have won, and everyone lost, the roundabout would start turning again, and the swings swinging.

Will it be any different this time?

Every year, according to the Press, the Labour Party is in the process of breaking up. "The Labour Party is in grave and imminent danger of destroying itself" wrote the *Sunday Times*; "The Labour Party is in a desperate position" declares the *News Chronicle*. This is all nonsense. As a vote-catching machine the Labour Party can still command more than ten million votes compared with the two million of the up-and-coming Liberals, whose conferences are marked by unity, unanimity and unbounded love for their debonair leader. Why?

The voting public is not influenced by the rows that take place at Labour Party conferences, in which, generally, differences over foreign policy are used as the setting for the struggle for power within the party to be played out. Most people are interested neither in foreign policy nor the internal struggles of the political parties. When elections come along they combine a political conservatism with what they consider to be self-interest, and vote accordingly. There can surely be no other explanation for the more or less consistent pattern of voting at the elections — including the consistent failure of the Liberals to make any headway.

What happened at Scarborough last week will leave no scars on the professional politicians. They will just carry on as before as the official opposition to the Government until the next general election, when everybody concerned will be full of the party spirit and united on the most important of all activities: vote-catching. As for the Bomb . . . the less said about it the better!

(October 15, 1960)

1961

SIT-DOWN — WITHOUT ILLUSIONS

The participants at today's sit-down in Whitehall will include a number of anarchists, most of whom, we suspect, are joining in the demonstration more out of a feeling of solidarity than because they cherish any illusions such as that the government will take notice of their demand that they should "immediately" scrap the Polaris agreement with the U.S. On the other hand, the government may well make a note of the demonstrators' declaration that "they can no longer stand aside while preparations are being made for the destruction of mankind".

But today's demonstration, at least the sit-down part of it, though symbolically it may do all these things, in reality resolves itself into a demonstration against the laws on obstruction, and a trial of strength between the law-breakers and the police, and it is to that aspect of the demonstration which the Press and Radio will, if at all, give the headlines.

Bertrand Russell in a letter to the Press declares that

> we have been driven to a policy of civil disobedience by the lack of representation or the misrepresentation of the policy of unilateralists in the organs of public information. Broadcasting and television are practically closed to us. It is difficult, almost impossible, to get articles or even letters into the daily papers. Most of the press has gone over to Authority — possibly in fear of being, otherwise, gobbled up.

And he goes on to argue that while all sorts of legal methods should continue to be employed, other methods must be used which have "news value" and will make it possible for the legal methods to "carry their full weight". In other words, only by civil disobedience — in this case the four-hour sit-down in Whitehall — will the Press take notice of the unilateralists' case, and that "only by such means can the barrier of ignorance and indifference" concerning this point of view be broken down.

Bertrand Russell is probably right when he says that the public in general is ignorant of the facts supporting the unilateralists' case, but even assuming that the organs of mass communications made amends, there are no grounds for assuming that this knowledge will break down the other "barrier": of indifference. We are not saying that the sit-down demonstration is a waste of time. What we are saying is that it is a mistake to assume as so many do nowadays, who are the backbone of the sit-down demonstrations, marches, picketings, fastings, etc., that *this* is "real action" and everything else from publishing papers and addressing small meetings or attending discussions, etc., are academic, intellectual, and a sheer waste of time.

In fact the demonstrations, etc., are simply other forms of propaganda which depend for their success not only on mass support but above all on publicity by the organs of mass communications. It is surely true to say that the Aldermaston March now receives less publicity from the Press in spite of the fact that as a demonstration it has grown in size each year. To what extent growing support for the March so far has been the result of propaganda by the marchers themselves among their friends and workmates or the result of Press publicity is difficult to ascertain.

Our guess is that it is the former and for the simple reason that the indirect propaganda we can expect for a cause through the publicity it receives in the daily Press is the result of a fleeting "splash" in one day's issue — a splash which is but a drop in an ocean of daily "splashes" which are so indiscriminate that a gory murder or a juicy sex case will invariably make a bigger "splash" as well as a bigger impact on the minds and in the conversation of the mass-fed public, than the serious issues of nuclear disarmament or the cold war. On the other hand the kind of propaganda which is conveyed by word of mouth in the day-to-day contacts we all have with friends and the people we work with, or through the regular publication of independent organs of ideas, reaches a smaller public but the chances that its effect will be more radical and lasting are infinitely greater.

It is surely unnecessary for us to point out that anarchists are very much in favour of movements which are prepared to engage in acts of civil disobedience. But whereas the Committee of 100 are principally concerned with the non-violent aspect of their actions

(Bertrand Russell writes: "The demonstration is to be non-violent, and any individual who allows himself to become violent will be disowned by the Committee")

we anarchists consider that the chances of success depend much more on the firm conviction that all governments are an obstacle to the creation of a world society based on co-operation and understanding, and in which any real differences between men will be settled by discussion and not force. Government is authority from above; and that authority can only be maintained by the use, or the threat, of force. Force is the language of government and it is therefore utopian to hope that it may be persuaded into believing that its message will be more convincing if it sheds its armour.

A movement of civil disobedience to achieve something positive must strike at the roots of power. If it's the law of obstruction that we are fighting against, by all means let's squat in the middle of Piccadilly Circus in our thousands when the police behave as they did during the picketing of South Africa House, or as they have done towards literature sellers in Hyde Park and elsewhere. If it's the control of the Press by a handful of tycoons or trusts that we want to break down we must encourage a mass boycott of the Press (assuming we cannot persuade journalists, printers and distributors to refuse to write, print and distribute for the monopolists) and at the same time set about producing newspapers to replace them.

If we want this country to disarm it is only by directing our efforts to the workers in the armaments industry — not to the government — that we may hope to succeed. To sit down outside the Defence Ministry is what Herbert Read in an article in *Peace News* (20/1/61) called "instinctive" action. We may feel all the better for it — and some we know, are hoping that they will be selected by the police to spend the night in the cells — but the charge will be for obstruction and not for threatening the State.

But if we paused to give a little more thought to our generous "instincts" then we should start by squatting in our thousands outside the factories producing the missiles and the planes and the bombs and all the electronic and other paraphernalia that comprise the modern war "machine". We should, in persuading the workers and scientists and technologists engaged in the perfection of annihilation of the anti-social aspects of their activities, offer not only arguments but a wilingness to share with them our last crust of bread until such time as they are able to secure other employment. But assuming that our arguments fail we should also be prepared to deny them entry to their factories of death. And if they object that we are preventing them from earning their living, or charge that in the name of freedom we are denying them theirs — of choosing the kind of job they will do — we must have the courage of our convictions and declare that we have no objection to their working for their own destruction but that we have a right to defend ourselves when their work not only threatens them with annihilation but also those of us who want *to live*.

Just as the employer has no *unchallenged* right to a privileged existence at the expense of those he employs, neither has a worker the right to engage in work which threatens the lives of others as well as his own, without, at least, their prior acquiescence. But neither can those of us who seek to persuade them to abandon that work, rely on moral argument *if* we are not, at the same time, prepared to cushion the economic sacrifices we are also expecting them to make for the cause of peace, by sharing our wage packets with them.

> "We must release the imagination of the people so that they become fully conscious of the fate that is threatening them, and we can best reach their imagination by our actions, by our fearlessness, by our liberty, and even our lives to the end that mankind shall be delivered from pain and suffering and universal death".

With these words Herbert Read concluded his *Peace News* "Protest Against Polaris" article. Fine words, fine sentiments, but in the circumstances, it all rings a bit phoney! Herbert Read is right when he declares that "the statesmen and scientists of the world have forfeited all moral authority". But are the *intellectuals* in any better moral position to criticise?

Let us cite an example where we have direct experience. For more than two decades we have been trying to build up a free press, free in the sense that in content it should be a forum for ideas outside the confines of the Establishment. Like Herbert Read we believe in releasing the "imagination of the people", confident that this, and not party lines, will lead to a libertarian way of thinking and living. When we have approached the writers and intellectuals who had something to say, the almost universal excuse for not writing for a paper such as FREEDOM has been that their time was limited, and it seemed to them that what time they had was better spent writing for the capitalist Press, for the "unconverted" public.

Apart from the cynical, but realistic, reflection that the capitalist Press also pays handsomely and FREEDOM doesn't, our objection to this argument is that so long as intellectuals of integrity write for the capitalist Press and ignore the independent, free press, the set-up will remain unchanged. Herbert Read put it very well in *Anarchy and Order* when he wrote

> The existing social order is outrageously unjust, and if we do not revolt against it, we are either morally insensitive or criminally selfish. *But if all that our revolt secures is merely a reconstruction of the societal crystal along another axis, our action has been in vain. There has been no chemical change.* (Our italics.)

If tomorrow the capitalist Press gave more space to unilateral disarmament, or even to anarchism this would not represent a revolution in the Press. It would still be in the hands of a few people whose principal interest was to make money and to maintain the system which protected them at all costs, including the freedom of the Press.

Now if writers are not prepared to make material "sacrifices" to boycott the yellow press and to build the free press, what impact do they think such high-sounding platitudes as "willingness to sacrifice our comfort, our liberty and even our lives" has on the average reader?

Indeed we hope that today's sit-down protesters have been influenced by other considerations than the adulation of the "big names". We hope that, in the first place, they have been moved by a feeling of solidarity, the kind of solidarity which in the last war induced many anarchists to register as COs in spite of the fact that they could not and did not recognise the competence of the Tribunals to assess their "consciences". Secondly we hope that they have taken part in this demonstration without any illusions as to its chances of bringing pressure on the government to change its policies. Thirdly we hope they have no illusions that the Press will be influenced by their willingness to go to prison, to accept and interpret their arguments. The Press defends the Establishment even when, like the *Guardian*, it exists "in the public interest". Fourthly we hope that they will not look upon sitting on a pavement in Whitehall for four hours as the cure-all for the problems of mankind. It's not governments that we must seek to change but the way of thinking among our fellow humans, and this is a long-term task which demands unremitting effort.

"But in the meantime mankind may well be annihilated". Undoubtedly the risk does exist. But the risk also exists that we will be so obsessed with the task of preventing mankind from being annihilated by an H-Bomb war, that we will overlook the fact that every day of the week thousands of people are dying in Africa, in Asia, in Europe and the Americas, by such conventional weapons as bombing planes, and flame-throwing tanks, in old-established institutions such as concentration camps and prisons or even of the oldest of mankind's complaints . . . starvation. For all these unfortunates death means annihilation. So far as they are concerned there is little consolation that their death does not in fact mean the annihilation of mankind. Who, other than the condemned man who sees no way of escape or the demagogue, who has no intention of dying for mankind, would be prepared to declare that the survival of mankind is more important than his own life?

For the past fifteen years we have lived in the "shadow" of a nuclear bomb that might "at any moment" plunge the world into darkness. For fifteen years we have been exhorted to do something about that specific problem; fifteen wasted years in which people might have spent their time more usefully tackling the problems and rejecting the values which have landed us in a world whose destruction requires only that one man should press one button. Do you think it possible?

(February 18, 1961)

DRESS REHEARSAL — OR SHOW-DOWN?

So far as "forcing the government's hand" on the issues of Polaris bases in Scotland the sit-down on February 18th can be written off as a failure. But then who among the demonstrators really expected the government to take notice of the Committee of 100 when it could virtuously point to the political "Left" for support in its nuclear weapons policies? So no political illusions. But as a spontaneous, human demonstration it was an overwhelming success. When 2,000 people say they will turn up to take part in the sit-down and in fact more than 4,000 as well as thousands of supporters turn up, in spite of a press silence which was significant, then all concerned can feel well satisfied with the result of this first demonstration.

Without underestimating the work put into the initial organisation by Michael Randle (Secretary) and the Committee members, what must have struck any observer, hostile or friendly, was the informality, the "unorganised" nature of the demonstration which contrasted so favourably with those tight-lipped, party organised, regimented demonstrators which we, of an older generation, are all too familiar with, and disgusted by. What an impressive sight it was in Whitehall as the column of sit-downers, flanked by supporters, spread itself it seemed to the full width of Whitehall and advanced like a great wave towards Parliament Square. With the noise of traffic temporarily silenced one suddenly was aware of the sound of thousands of shuffling feet and voices in conversation, occasionally punctuated by the hysterical appeals from the loudspeaker of the one van and one Vespa counter-demonstration of the Empire

Loyalists. At Parliament Square they were joined by seedy youths marching Indian file and advertising their wares: Mosley's newspaper *Action*. As the column reached the Square it seemed as if the main concern of the few police on duty was to divert the traffic, but as soon as the demonstrators began to take their places on the pavement, hundreds of police suddenly emerged from their hide-outs in the side streets to encircle and contain the sit-down to the pavement around the Defence Ministry. But as the human chain wound itself round the three sides of the huge, ugly building, so the wall of police became merely isolated posts of a fence without wires.

Two sides of the building were already filled and the column from Trafalgar Square was still advancing when four fire engines, bells clanging, suddenly descended on Great George Street. Serious-faced fire-chiefs consulted with serious-faced police-chiefs — as if they hadn't discussed it all beforehand! — and we can imagine that other police-chiefs were observing closely the reactions of the squatting demonstrators. We observed them too; no one stirred, a few jokes were made about the wisdom of bringing a raincoat to such demonstrations, and ten minutes later the fire-engines with their police-aides slunk off, their bells muffled, their hoses dry, to look for a different conflagration.

The Press reacted with indifference or hostility, and in the case of the *Sunday Times* with alarm. Neither the *Sunday Times* nor *The Observer*, nor the *Guardian* and *The Times* on the Monday, committed themselves to an editorial comment. The *Pictorial* came out with one of its pungent comments which just shows that even if Mr King inhabits the lofty heights of monopoly his reporters have their ears to the ground.

> The *Sunday Pictorial* certainly believes that their ideas are wrong, but we defend their right to be wrong . . . At least the demonstrators feel strongly enough about an urgent issue to DO something. One trouble with politics these days is that they are too limp and unexciting. Few people care deeply enough to get out and crusade for what they believe to be right. There are too many "don't knows", "don't cares". At least Earl Russell and his Whitehall Warriors can claim that squatting on the pavement is better than sitting on the fence.

The *Sunday Telegraph* on the other hand issued a warning of the dangers (to the authority of the State of course) in allowing such demonstrations to take place without opposition. Bertrand Russell and his friends were not charming eccentrics nor the dedicated representatives of a persecuted minority. On the contrary they belonged to a "highly organised political movement" which in a few years had achieved "immense political success by normal methods of persuasion". Aldermaston and similar outings were now OK demonstrations. But, warns the *Sunday Telegraph*

> if many more of these — now numbering many thousands — who support Lord Russell's views were to adopt his methods national safety as well as public order would be seriously in danger.
>
> No man can be denied the right to resist violently or non-violently the policies which his conscience instructs him to resist; but no one who chooses this course can claim that society should not oppose him. Demonstrations like yesterday's must be restrained with just as little and just as much force as is necessary to stop them spreading into a public danger.

The *Sunday Telegraph* is right, and as if to confirm its fears, at the Press conference called by the Committee of 100 last Sunday, Bertrand Russell declared that the demonstration of February 18 was only a "dress rehearsal" for future "more positive" action "such as the authorities cannot tolerate". And in last week's *Peace News* Michael Scott shows that the implications of civil disobedience have been understood, at least by him, when he writes

> We shall resist not only the threat of war but the evils of oppression and criminal neglect of the great resources of the earth through exploiting and restrictive practices. We shall resist these abuses whether within the system of so-called Communism or of capitalism and colonialism.

In other words, when one embarks on civil disobedience one is not simply seeking to persuade government on a specific issue such as unilateral nuclear disarmament; one is challenging the authority of the State, the system of government and the existing values of society. This means — to quote Michael Scott's conclusions

> that a great deal of new thinking has to be done and done quickly. For many of the ideas we have inherited are totally inadequate to meet the great menace and dilemma of mankind in the fields of religion, politics, ethics and economics. The epoch making changes that we have lived through have created a totally new situation which can only be dealt with by new ideas. The threat of force has been removed as the ultimate sanction.

Such arrangements not only alarm the thinking Right, but the leaders and would-be leaders on the so-called Left as well. The reactions of the three weekly organs of the Left — the *Spectator*, the *New Statesman* and *Tribune* — to the sit-down are illuminating. Last week's *Spectator* ignored the demonstration altogether. The *New Statesman* ignored it editorially, having the previous week published the following editorial note over Bertrand Russell's article on Civil Disobedience:

> This week-end Bertrand Russell and other demonstrators who accept the tactic of civil disobedience will take part in an unlawful protest against the Polaris missile in

particular and nuclear policy in general. For reasons stated at length in this journal last week we do not believe that either his assumptions or the tactics he advocates are correct in present circumstances, but we believe that he should have a full opportunity to explain his position.

But even more interesting is the reaction of *Tribune* which for many socialists is the movement's white hope in the struggle against the revisionists and the deviationists of the Party. *Tribune* gave no advance publicity to the demonstration, and last week in an editorial on "Civil Disobedience and CND" came down solidly on the side of the Establishment. "Everyone who has grasped the barest outline of the arguments (of the advocates of civil disobedience) must have sympathy for the resolute and unselfish character of their actions". But

those who favour civil disobedience cast doubt on the effectiveness of political action to change the immediate course of Governmental policy. And, indeed, they regard such action as quite secondary to personal non-violent protest.

There are two great dangers which are apparent in such a policy. First, that the argument as such against nuclear weapons (which is enormously powerful — it won at Labour's conference at Scarborough last year) is not materially advanced by such actions; second that it injures people's belief in the effectiveness of democratic action.

The reasons for this are quite simple. Any protest against nuclear strategy which an individual makes cannot possibly be left at that point. For once one challenges the assumption of such strategy, one is faced with a whole series of other decisions that have to be made.

These budding politicians have put their finger on the spot, but whereas they look upon it as the weakness of the civil disobedience movement, to our minds it is its ultimate strength assuming that it proceeds along the lines outlined by Michael Scott. For *Tribune* the difference between the measures of civil disobedience and the Aldermaston March is that

civil disobedience is an end in itself — not a means (as is the Aldermaston March) to achieving an end.

Only politicians could make the distinction as *Tribune* does. As we see it, they have got the wrong end of the stick! The Aldermaston March has indeed become an end in itself, for so far as achieving any change in government policy is concerned it has miserably failed. After three marches not only have we still got the bomb but we are also about to receive the Polaris depot ship and submarines in the waters of Holy Loch. The realists among the supporters of CND seem to have drawn conclusions which *Tribune* and other politically blinkered Establishment "socialists" cannot allow themselves to see.

Civil disobedience may well be an unthinking act of despair among otherwise law-abiding citizens, and they undoubtedly will think before joining any further demonstration. But a determined, conscious movement of civil disobedience seeks to upset the smooth running machine of centralised power, of injustice, of rule of the many by the few, of permanent tension between nations and of production for profit and not for needs, not just for the sake of destroying that machine — we are no political Luddites — but because at long last it has dawned on some of our fellow beings that the machine of State, whoever operates it, and however good are the intentions of the operators, cannot function in any other way than the one for which it was designed.

For instance, the only realistic approach to unilateral nuclear disarmament — realistic that is, from the point of view of influencing government policy — is that adopted by people like Commander King-Hall who argue that from a military point of view this country would be stronger if it spent its limited resources — compared with those of America and Russia — on other kinds of weapons and defence. Such an approach does not put a spanner in the machine of state; on the contrary it seeks to strengthen it! It is not, therefore, a contribution to peace, but at most a cunning, unorthodox, move in the game of power politics. The foundation of force on which the machine of state is bedded remains, unscathed, unshattered; if anything the machine has been oiled to run more smoothly.

A movement of civil disobedience, as we see it, is a movement of thinking individuals who can no longer accept that their lives should be regulated and disposed of by a machine called the state or government. We are individuals, not holes in a card to be fed into an electronic computer

> *(Incidentally, it was one of the warming and exciting sights of the sit-down demonstration that it was not a blancmange of humanity but a turbulent sea of faces, young and old, smooth and wrinkled, smiling and serious, tense and carefree; each declaring his individuality and at the same time wanting to be, and accepting the responsibility of being, a link in that chain of solidarity and protest.)*

and as thinking, reasoning individuals we demand to organise our own lives in the knowledge that we can do so while at the same time identifying ourselves with the needs and dreams of those around us. The goal of such a movement is to provide the environment in which men, women . . . and children, can develop as individual human beings. To this end they must seek to destroy the machinery of centralised authority, the state, government, élites. Civil disobedience cuts the grass from under the feet of budding politicians, undermines the authority of government and the confidence of its henchmen, the police, as well as building up the confidence and sense of responsibility of the individuals engaged in such action. "Unity is strength" but the unity we seek is not in numbers but unity through diversity, the unity which is built on mutual respect and not on sameness.

(March 4, 1961)

ON THE MARCH

This Easter week-end, for the fourth successive year, many people will be spending their holidays on the march. In spite of the fact that this year the number of participants will be higher than ever, that London will be approached by two columns instead of one (a brilliant innovation), the impact of the first march on the public imagination cannot be repeated. That first march, because it was the first, was unpredictable, and its destination *was* the centre of nuclear power in this country. Anything might have happened when the marchers got there. Even as a symbolic gesture it had more meaning than subsequent marches which have concentrated on London, "centre of political power which controls Aldermaston". For everybody knows that governments can come and go but the Woolwich Arsenals, the Aldermastons and the Vickers Armstrongs go on for ever.

In other words, Aldermaston marches are very successful methods of letting off steam without upsetting the *status quo*. They are as respectable as May Day demonstrations and Trades Unions; all part of the Establishment if they can hold out long enough doing the same thing. Like Rights of Way they can, by an annual formality, be accepted as part of our daily lives.

But what the unilateralists are trying to do, surely, is to change the pattern of political life since they are proposing (*a*) that the British government should conduct its international business with arguments and moral example and not the threat of force and (*b*) that governments should be influenced by the will of the people.

Perhaps Canon Collins can be said to have lived, politically speaking, a cloistered life, and such illusions are excusable (though after four years he should have learned *something* about politics). But the Kingsley Martins, the J.B. Priestleys and the A.J.P. Taylors are really too old in the tooth, politically, to have any excuses for believing, or suggesting to others, that governments are amenable to argument or considerations of humanity. Is there not proof enough, when the Parliamentary Labour Party which professes all the brotherly love and internationalism which the Tories do not, is, even when not in office, unwilling to abide by the Party's Conference decisions on nuclear disarmament? Is it not, quite simply, that a politician who aspires to positions of power in politics cannot think in terms other than the conventional ones, whereby, though the people elect their "representatives", force is the only language they will respect when it comes to running the country.

Similarly "diplomacy" without the argument of force is as utopian as the concept of "democracy" without the police and MI5. A fact of life which the late-lamented Nye Bevan was the first to accept once he had sampled the fruits of office. It must not be overlooked that when Mr Bevan declared, at the Labour Party Conference of 1957, that for Britain to scrap her stocks of nuclear weapons would mean "that you will send the British Foreign Secretary naked into the conference chamber" he was not in fact Foreign Secretary but merely the nominee of the Labour *Shadow* Cabinet. That is, he was gratuituously telling the country what his position would be if he were in office even without the "responsibilities" of office. It is notorious that politicians are more radical (or less reactionary) in opposition than in power. If on the question of nuclear disarmament the Parliamentary Labour Party in opposition is so reactionary that it is prepared to expel five of its members for dividing the House on the debate on Estimates for the Armed Forces (on the grounds that by so doing they were saying that they would be prepared for the country to be totally disarmed — an unthinkable situation to be in!), what could the CND hope from the Labour Party if they were *in power*?

Indeed this is one of the major dilemmas of the CND which though directing its protest to the government, in fact seeks to convert the Labour Party to a unilateralist position. And the more successful it is in its efforts the more certain is it of splitting the Party and ensuring that it fails to win the next general election. It is, indeed, ironical that the chances of a popular movement succeeding get smaller as its numbers grow, but only if one believes that governments are impressed by numbers or that the system we live under conforms to the dictionary definition of democracy.

If we rule out the Aldermaston Annual Outing as useless what do we suggest should be done? We only say that the Aldermaston marches are useless *so far as removing the threat of annihilation of mankind by nuclear warfare is concerned*. We are too modest as to our own efforts, as anarchist publicists, to decry the efforts of others. But there is this important difference between us. Whereas CND seeks to *influence* government by mass support we seek mass support for our ideas in order to *weaken* government. In other words, we are interested in influencing people, not governments. We are concerned with people taking initiative and not with wasting their time seeking to prompt governments to take initiatives on their behalf.

Undoubtedly, it will not be possible to abolish government and authority overnight; but we only strengthen governments and the state by assuming or expecting that these institutions can satisfactorily represent or express our wishes and aspirations. Only by assuming the responsibility *ourselves* can we withdraw the initiative from government.

In four years some supporters of CND have reached the point where not even the Committee of 100 will satisfy their demands. The dilemma of the unilateral disarmers is that while on the one hand they have a cause which has a popular appeal, on the other they are seeking to remove the main prop from under the edifice of government; indeed they are expecting the government to do the job for them in response to "popular demand".

Quite rightly the government argues that if you remove the main prop the whole edifice of government collapses, and apart from replying, as some unilateralists do, that the edifice can be propped up with conventional bombs, there is no answer *unless* one takes the anarchist position of "down with all governments". But in that case one has no faith in governments or politicians, and there is no point in directing one's appeals and efforts to persuading them to act on our behalf. Certainly one would not attack government at its strongest point. Rather one would seek to withdraw power from the government by encouraging the people themselves to form their own organisations of production and consumption, of services and of international relations. In other words, by taking over more and more of the initiative for running our own lives we will succeed in dispelling the universal belief in the necessity of government, which is to our minds the biggest stumbling block to any radical change in the organisation of society and the relations between peoples and nations.

We know this is, at best, a slow process. We know that for some impatient young people this is not doing anything whereas marching and sitting down is. Readers of FREEDOM know our views on marching and sitting-down. We always support positive expression of a people's feelings but if such manifestations are not to end in sterility and disillusionment it is essential to face the realities of such "action" and to point to the dead-end into which it leads.

The anarchist approach will take a long time, and in the meantime we may all be blown sky-high by the maniacs in power. The people of the world are in a position to prevent such a possibility since they both produce and handle these weapons of total destruction. Yet they do nothing about it, and to our minds they do nothing about it not because they are ignorant of the consequences of a nuclear war — everybody now knows what it would mean — but because they feel impotent to take any action which would be effective. In other words they are unaware of their own potential power as workers. Is it not obvious that if they had this awareness they could simply, by withdrawing their labour from all work connected even remotely with war preparations, paralyse government?

Four Aldermaston marches have sought to influence governments and create "pressure groups" within the Labour Party all to no avail. Is it not time that all the goodwill present at those demonstrations be used to persuade our fellow workers to refuse to sell their labour to the merchants of death?

(April 1, 1961)

A WELCOME TO ALL . . .

The *Evening Standard* in publishing a list of "Easter Monday attendance figures" showing that fewer people were at the Ban the Bomb rally in Trafalgar Square (32,000) than at either Goodwood races (45,000) or the football match at Stamford Bridge (60,000), implied, presumably, that more people were interested in one major football match than in the cause of nuclear disarmament. But why in that case did the Trafalgar Square rally dominate the *Evening Standard's* front page and spill over onto the centre spread and dominate that too?

There can be no doubt that one does not have to sympathise with the objectives of the CND in order to be impressed and moved by demonstrations such as last week's march, or the sit-down in February. For unlike the 60,000 football fans who are *spectators* at a performance of 22 "stars", those who take part in these marches are both the actors and the spectators in a moving demonstration of solidarity. As one BBC commentator put it, the reward for the marchers was the "rare experience of sharing something with so many others".

And whilst Aldermaston marches will not move governments they are a kind of annual general meeting at which members feed their faith and encourage others to join them. We do not say this sneeringly. Would that the anarchists could hold a four-day rally of anarchists and sympathisers a tenth of the size!

This year, however, infiltration of the CND by Communists and fellow-travellers was most noticeable. This year, for the first time, banners of political parties were much more in evidence. The argument for including the banners of branches of political parties and Trade Unions is that since the CND seeks to bring about its programme by constitutional means: that is, by influencing parliament and the government in power, the more support they get from the political parties the greater their chances. On the other hand the case for excluding the Communist Party is, to our minds, a strong one.

Quite apart from the widespread prejudice evoked in the minds of the public in general and more often than not for the wrong reason to any initiative or movement which is sponsored or supported by the Communists, we believe that many sincere radicals who would be prepared to work with people of many different political, and religious affiliations on determined issues, would be unwilling to do so if it also meant joining with members of the Communist Party. And for the reason that one cannot trust a party, or its supporters, which owes blind allegiance to the Russian regime and supports or opposes government, initiatives, policies and principles only at the behest of the Soviet leadership. Such a party is without principle and unreliable.

Its attitude to the CND is a case in point. Up to last year the Communist party leadership was opposed to its members taking part (whether it was because they were not allowed to carry their party banners on the march, or whether they were afraid their members might be contaminated by contact with the pacifists and non-party radicals, we do not know). But already last year the Communists were more in evidence as a Party. this year they were right in. By next year will they have wormed their way into the top places of the CND? However ambitious Canon Collins and his friends may be, when it comes to the political game of infiltration they are babes so far as the Communists are concerned. In an interview with the Canon published in last Saturday's *Daily Worker* he said:

> We do not affiliate with, or have affiliated with us, any other organisation. But we accept with pleasure the support of any individuals or groups who genuinely share our concern *and wish our party to succeed* . . . We welcome them all *and we assume that they come on the march to prosper our cause.* (Our italics.)

Support from the Communist Party, far from "prospering" a cause is a kiss of death as so many independent movements in the past have learned to their cost. The CND is in many respects a movement of people who are disillusioned with party politics and in particular is this true of the young supporters of the campaign who, says the Canon, not only are interested in politics but want "to release themselves from the threat (of the bomb) and play their part in seeing that the world survives". But, he added, "They feel that existing organisations including the political parties, lack sincerity and purpose".

This is a state of mind which neither the Labour Party nor the Communists can approve of, and with all parties desperately seeking the formula which will attract youth to their ranks one can well imagine that the party managers are less concerned with the objectives of the CND than with its potentialities as a source for recruiting members. But equally they might well consider that the more successful CND is in its development as a rank-and-file movement of protest the less faith will the new generation have in the party machines, and in that case their interest in CND would be to see how to smash it. So far as the Communists are concerned, the easiest way to halt the CND's progress is to penetrate it *en masse*.*

The Press, the Labour politicians and the government will then be able to point the accusing finger at CND and declare that it is a CP dominated body. And the movement will die, in spite of increased numbers, simply because it will have been robbed of its main assets: its independence, its spontaneity and its integrity.

These assets not even the hacks and pimps of Fleet Street can write-off in their otherwise superficial accounts of the Easter marches. These are the assets which the *Evening Standard* editor could not ignore, and surely explain why he could compare the Trafalgar Square demonstration unfavourably with a football crowd and yet consider it the most important feature story for his front and middle pages.

Support from the Communist Party might swell the numbers — for a time. But one thing is certain, that the assets to which we have referred, and which account for the uniqueness of the Campaign for Nuclear Disarmament, would be lost for good. And this would be a pity: not because we have illusions about CND achieving its declared aims but because as at present constituted it encourages the kind of individual responsibility which thinking people may well come to link with the anarchist rejection of all governments and all political tutelage.

(April 8, 1961)

THE PEOPLE IN THE STREET

Last Saturday's sit-down demonstration in London, apart from a disappointing drop in the numbers who took part must surely be considered a success for all concerned. A success for the demonstrators who, faced with their first test of mass arrests, "stood" their ground with very few exceptions to await the conse-

---

* It was noticeable that the youth sections of the march had more than a sprinkling of Communist Youth. Some observers with whom we discussed this aspect of the march went so far as to say that the CP dominated the youth sections. And yet the total membership of the Young Communist League as declared at the CP Congress last week was 2,500 for the whole of Britain. It would therefore seem that a very large proportion of the YCL was on the march last week-end.

quences whatever they might have been; a success for the police whose counter-demonstration was as impressive as the demonstration itself; a success for the State which through its Courts vindicated the LAW as well as frustrating the marchers' intentions to reach Parliament Square. But before examining these successes, let us first state the facts since some of the Press reports were more wide of the mark than usual. It is true that the Press was also harried by the police who were determined to seal off the demonstrators from the public. That the Press, which has access to the battlefields and the Royal Presence, should have been kept at a distance from a non-violent sit-down in the heart of London, must be taken as a compliment, as an indication that the forces of law and order were taking us seriously at last.

The *Observer* report noted that there were 1,200 demonstrators. Why their reporters should have thought this it is difficult to say. Police estimates were 2,500. Some observers put the number at 3,000, others at 2,000. The numbers arrested according to the *Sunday Telegraph* were "more than 1,000". The official figures were 826. According to the same paper the Metropolitan Police Commissioner had "at least 1,000 of the Force's strength of 17,000 at his immediate disposal". But it was obvious even to the least expert observer that there were many more than that. (More than an hour before the Square meeting started hundreds of police had been disgorged by coaches and vans, and by three o'clock they were lining Whitehall, Parliament Square and still further, past the House of Lords.) Indeed, the *Observer* which had only seen 1,200 sit-downers, saw "2,000 of them (police) lining Whitehall, blocking its opening into Parliament Square and crowding in the courts and side streets off the route" and a further 1,000 were on call.

There were two halts along Whitehall, the first of short duration, and we have heard no explanation for it. The second, it was announced, would last ten minutes. Senior police officials it appears approached the leaders of the march with the offer of a compromise. One newspaper reported that it consisted in allowing a symbolic sit-down on the pavement in Parliament Square of 50 marchers. The *Observer's* version was that "if the marchers promised not to sit in the road — to keep to the central garden of the square — to keep off the grass, they might proceed". According to Michael Randle, secretary of the Committee of 100, the police offer was to allow marchers to proceed in batches of 50 to occupy the pavements around the garden in Parliament Square.

The offer was refused, and the leaders were informed that they would be prevented from proceeding further. By then the ranks of

The first Committee of 100 sit down demonstration February 18 1961 advances along Whitehall headed by, among others, from l. to r. George Clark, Vic Richardson, Bertrand Russell, Michael Randle.

I. Sitting-Down

25 Ralph Schoenman addresses the meeting in Trafalgar Square before the sit-down at the Defence Ministry.

26 Part of the huge crowd in Trafalgar Square February 18 1961.

27 The octagenarian philosopher Bertrand Russell addresses the demonstration on February 18. On the Nelson column plinth, from l. to r.: George Clark, a nuclear scientist, Herbert Read (in beret), Hugh MacDiarmid (in kilt), Lady Russell, Mrs Kerr (Labour MP), Michael Randle, Ralph Schoenman.

28 Trafalgar Square February 18 1961.

29 Trafalgar Square Feb 18 1961.

Sit-down at Ministry of Defence February 18 1961. l. to r. M. Randle, Michael Scott, Bertrand Russell, Helen Allegranza.

31

32

February 1
1961 sit-do
Ministry of
Defence.

33

34

April 29 1961 sit-down in Parliament Square. Marshalls rallying demonstrators for the march along Whitehall.

36 And in Whitehall a reception committee awaits the marchers to prevent them from reaching Parliament Square.

37 The police cordon cannot obscure completely the Cenotaph, that reminder of the Great War to end Wars.

38 A smiling sit-downer symbolically tests the cordon. *They* are not amused.

the marchers had been closed and flanked on both sides by policemen standing shoulder to shoulder. We were trapped encircled by a chain which could not be broken except by violence, and because the Committee of 100 is pledged to a campaign of non-violent protest the only answer was to sit down in the roadway. Within a few minutes everyone was uncomfortably seated (it was a mistake, when the march was halted, for the demonstrators to bunch up together as closely as they did. For apart from the discomfort when sitting, the task of the police when they came to pick up the sitters was made easier since it was difficult to "go limp" in the uncomfortable sitting up position everybody had to adopt because of the lack of leg room). A police car then moved along the line of sitters warning them that they were committing an offence, and shortly afterwards, since the only reaction to the warning was a wave of cheering, the vans and coaches moved in to load up their cargo of human protest. Starting at the extremities of the column, the police first removed the Committee leaders; they then took sample loads at various spots along the column. As our fellow-protesters were driven off they were given a loud cheer from the roadway as well as from spectators on the pavement on the other side of the road. This went on for nearly one and a half hours; then one saw two empty coaches arrive presumably to load up more law-breakers. But they didn't. What happened then, according to the *News of the World*, was that

> Dozens of police moved among the remaining squatters taking names and addresses and warning them that if they stayed seated they would be arrested. Most of them moved on to the pavement to avoid detention.

This is a naked lie! The police may have taken names and given warnings, though this did not happen in the vicinity of the writer. What did happen instead, was that the police, starting from the Trafalgar Square end, began to pick up the sitters and carry or drag them to the pavement and dump them there. At one stage in the operation a certain amount of rough handling took place, with the police actually throwing their limp human bundles onto people who had already been dumped on the pavement. One demonstrator, who turned out to be a Justice of the Peace, rose to ask an Inspector for his name (since the hierarchy of the Force do not wear their badge of slavery on their shoulders as does, for instance PC G.434 who many of us thought was throwing people about with a little too much gusto). The Inspector simply refused to give it and walked off. So far from being intimidated by the 800 arrests and by threats of further arrests, no one left the roadway on his feet. Everyone had to be removed by the police. Once on the pavement the police *cordon sanitaire* was re-formed, shoulder to shoulder they were, and we were then informed that we were at liberty to stay until the end of the demonstration, *that we were not under arrest*, and that anyone who wished could leave. So far as we could see 1.0 one vacated his or her piece of pavement, apart from one or two hopeless attempts to get through the police cordon to the roadway. At 5.45 pm the demonstrators made their way back to Trafalgar Square through a funnel of policemen, and there they dispersed. These are the facts of the demonstration last Sunday.

Now, let us examine what at the outset we called the "successes". First, the police "success". Undoubtedly the police high-ups and the Home Secretary, Mr Rab Butler, in the light of the magnitude and homogeneity of the February 18th sit-down viewed the second demonstration with some apprehension. Obviously it was not a traffic problem that was worrying them. It is also clear that the Home Secretary did not fear that we were on the threshold of the social revolution. But Authority, whether it calls itself Tory or Socialist, cannot allow its authority to be flouted and challenged by the people, for the very simple reason that to defend it, it relies on, say, one per cent force and 99 per cent acquiescence, apathy or bluff (which includes *fear* of the consequences arising from flouting the law). The strength of demonstrations, such as those organised by the Committee of 100, lies less in the mass support they receive than in the willingness and ability of those engaged in them, to pursue their objectives *in spite of* the sanctions of the law. That high police officials should have, last Saturday, shown willingness to reach a compromise arrangement with the Committee is both an acknowledgement of their respect for the demonstrators' determination and integrity, as well as an admission of the impotence of the Executive when challenged. Not by a pin-striped, House-trained opposition "on the benches opposite", playing the game according to the rules (mutually agreed, for their own protection, as politicians) but by the people . . . in the streets.

We try, to the best of our ability, to base our opinions on evidence not wishful thinking. The facts so far as last Saturday's sit-down is concerned are that (*a*) there were probably 2,000 fewer demonstrators than at the previous sit-down, that is about half; (*b*) the authorities, sharing the Committee's optimism, reckoned on there being 3,000 more demonstrators than in fact there were and laid their plans accordingly; (*c*) in spite of the fact that the Commissioner of the Metropolitan Police based his personnel requirements on the assumption that there would be 5,000 and not 2,500 demonstrators, yet in the middle of Whitehall he is prepared to negotiate a face-saving alternative; (*d*) this being refused by the Committee of 100 the police had to start arresting people on a mass scale or lose face; (*e*) but the moment they do so, other machinery is set in motion; the people arrested must be taken into custody, charged, searched and appear before a magistrate within 24 hours. It may involve having to spend the night in custody, which adds to the administrative problems.

It was quite clear last Saturday that in carrying out what the *News of the World* headlined "The Greatest Mass Arrest of the Century" they had bitten off more than the courts could chew. It would only have needed a plan of non-co-operation — such as refusing to give one's name, pleading not guilty, insisting that the actual policeman who carried out the arrest should give evidence — to have given the machinery of Law and Order chronic indigestion. As it was certain legal formalities were by-passed at the police stations and by the Courts in order to deal with what were, after all, good-humoured prisoners.

It would seem, from the evidence last Saturday, that had there been 5,000 sit-downers, even with the large police force on duty, they would not have been able to clear the roadway within the time-limit of the demonstration. But of course we do not doubt that the police have many more tricks up their sleeves to deal with future demonstrations.

So far as the State's "success" is concerned, it is clear to us that the government was anxious to vindicate its authority without having to resort to methods which would spotlight the demonstration, and in this sense its success — in having the roads cleared — was at the same time a failure in that it was done by means which resulted in the biggest publicity the unilateralists have received to date.

So far as the success of the demonstration is concerned, there can be no doubt that in spite of smaller numbers, and in spite of the fact that Parliament Square was not reached the demonstrators were tested and came out of the test stronger and more determined. But it seems to us that a number of lessons have to be learned from the demonstration so far as tactics are concerned for future actions.

But because we believe that one lesson is that one cannot co-operate with the police, we do not propose to discuss in public what, in our opinion, future tactics should be. But it is obvious that a movement of civil disobedience and protest cannot achieve its objectives if it gives advance information to the "enemy" as to its programme thus handing over the initiative to the authorities every time.

Nevertheless with all its defects last Saturday's demonstration was an advance so far as the mood of the demonstrators was concerned.' Of the 18th February demonstration we wrote: "Sit-down — without illusions". Of the 29th April one is tempted to substitute "with hope", for perhaps for the first time many people became aware of the strength that lies in each of us when we start thinking and acting as individuals in a "community" of individuals. And let us not forget one important asset of these sit-downs: the comradeship that is forged by the people "in the streets".

(May 6, 1961)

AWAY FROM THE PARTIES!

Last week's *Tribune* in a short and sour editorial comment on the April 29 sit-down, attacks such demonstrations as "ineffectual" acts of civil disobedience which get publicity but this "is not the same thing as publicity for the argument against nuclear weapons". These arguments, declares *Tribune*

account for the spectacular success of the Campaign for Nuclear Disarmament. The Aldermaston marches have had their place in the campaign, but mainly as demonstrations of the growing body of support won at meetings and discussions all over the country.

Patient explanation won the TUC for unilateralism and found its culmination in the decision made at the Labour Party conference. But patience is not a quality that commends itself to the organisers of the Whitehall sit-down. Although getting rid of nuclear weapons *must* be a political decision they want to lead nuclear disarmers out of, not into, the political struggle.

Now, one cannot just write-off the *Tribune* criticisms of the Committee of 100 as worthless — even though one might think them dishonest. And those of us who take part in these demonstrations, at least, would welcome a clarification of the objectives, the direction, of the sit-downs. Are they intended to bring to the notice of the public the imminent dangers of nuclear war? If so then *Tribune* is right, for however much publicity was given to the last demonstration — a *Peace News* report estimates that it was more than for the last two Aldermastons put together — it was the kind of publicity which to our minds can hardly have advanced the cause of nuclear disarmament or unilateralism one jot. (And it is interesting to note that whereas most newspapers published more or less accurate accounts of the demonstration, the editorial columns maintained a deathly silence.)

Thus such demonstrations earn the disapproval both of the Press and the major political parties, as well as of the so-called progressive Left-wingers, is understandable. We are sure that the eloquence of the last sentence of the *Tribune* piece has not escaped our readers.

In that one sentence *Tribune* expresses all the fears of politicians, of all who have a stake in the maintenance of the political and social *status quo*.* As we were saying in these columns last week, the people "in the streets" upset both the powers-that-be and the aspirants to power more than all the petitions, and parliamentary "oppositions" and votes of censure put together.

We are not sure whether the Committee of 100 and some of its supporters are clear in their minds as to where such a movement leads. Or perhaps they do know but being committed to a campaign for unilateral disarmament have armed themselves with blinkers no less than those socialists who, having entered the political arena, no longer "see" the political realities around them which make it abundantly clear to everybody else that there will never be any socialism *via* the ballot box.

There was an interesting letter in last week's *Peace News* in which a woman reader seeks to distinguish between "relevant" and "irrelevant" civil disobedience. By the former the writer meant "that the passer-by can grasp that a protest is being made against modern war". On this basis she could understand demonstrations at rocket bases, and outside the Ministry of Defence. But "to sit down in Parliament Square seems to me irrelevant, and I doubt if publicity can overcome this weakness". And she concludes:

> Can Michael Randle tell me how I am to explain to intelligent and sympathetic onlookers the value of sitting down in *Parliament Square*; why, in fact I am wrong, if I am, in believing it to be irrelevant and therefore stupid?

To this Michael Randle (Secretary of the Committee of 100) replied agreeing that civil disobedience must be relevant to be effective, but adds that

> I am not convinced, however, that this means that only "direct action" at nuclear establishments and rocket bases is valid. Obstructions at symbolic points — the Defence Ministry, the Houses of Parliament — can also make their point.

---

* Note that not a single MP or TU leader took part in the sit-downs whereas a number joined in the Aldermaston marches.

Firstly we would make the point that any symbolic act whether it be that of a David Pratt or of 2,500 non-violent sit-downers courting arrest is not sufficient by itself, but needs its "propagandists", its interpreters. If therefore the relevance of sit-downs is to be grasped by the passer-by (or the public at large) almost as much attention should be paid to such mundane tasks as the distribution of leaflets to the passers-by as to the organisation of the sit-down,* bearing in mind that one cannot rest any hopes on the Press filling the role of faithful "interpreter" of one's act of "disobedience".

Secondly we would argue that a demonstration of "civil disobedience", valuable as it undoubtedly can be, in awakening public interest to specific issues, has an equally important psychological effect on the demonstrators themselves. And the authorities have not been slow in realising this. The facts speak for themselves: they honoured the Whitehall sit-down with a record police turn-out and a record number of arrests though the demonstrators were only a little more than half the number engaged in the first sit-down and but a fraction of those who participated in the Aldermaston and Wethersfield marches that made their way to London this year.

Their method was intimidation by mass arrest. And when the machine they relied on was choked, they found themselves obliged to carry each demonstrator from the road to the pavement, and accept the *fait accompli* that they were unequipped to prevent them from remaining seated on the pavement. Most of us, we think, were aware of the fact that they could then have tried to wash us away with the help of the Fire Brigade and that had we been in democratic France or in totalitarian Russia the police might have sprayed us with their sten guns (which probably explains why the French and the Russians do not normally protest by sitting-down?). The fact is that for reasons known to Mr Butler and the Police chiefs we were not washed away. Perhaps, once more they paid us the compliment of, this time, believing that we would refuse to be washed off the pavements?

By that time how many demonstrators were engaging in a demonstration against nuclear war and how many more were, instead, demonstrating against *authority* and for their dignity as human beings?

For this reason not only ourselves but many around us found the gratuitous remarks of some Marshals that "the police are only do-

---

* We confess to being a little shocked to learn that the last sit-down cost "about £1,000 to mount" (*Peace News* May 5). How much of this was spent in explaining the "relevance" of the demonstration to the public?

ing their job" more than irritating; and when the arrests and removals to the pavement had been completed that some demonstrators should chat and joke with the policemen showed a lack of understanding of the role the police play in the society against which these very people were supposed to be protesting.

After all, if we are prepared to excuse the policeman for being a policeman on the grounds that he is "only doing his job" then we must apologise for the General, the politician and the hangman as well as the soldier, airman and the workers in the armaments industry who are also only doing jobs which are considered essential to the well-being of society. If we haven't the courage to declare that *we know* what are anti-social occupations and activities and show our disapproval by refusing to have normal intercourse with those who engage in them, then we might as well give up sitting in the streets and buy a "telly" instead, and spend the rest of our lives sitting in front of that!

Michael Randle in his reply referred to above, declared that "there is also a case for more general obstruction and defiance in a society which is so closely geared to the production of nuclear weapons". A "case"? This sounds to us like the week's biggest understatement!

As a matter of fact our friend is wrong. Our society is geared to the production of Profits and Power. Nuclear weapons are only means to those ends. Assuming that you eliminate these horrors, States and power-hungry politicians will only resort to others. The tank, the flame-thrower and the A-Bomb may well be in the category of pea-shooters compared with the H-Bomb but it must not be forgotten that at some stage in technological "progress", they were "ultimate" weapons; the last word in destruction and "wickedness". Modern man, capitalist society, have always been "geared" to the most destructive weapons that science and industry could produce. There is no reason why the public at large should be more concerned with the weapon at the disposal of governments now, because it is an H-Bomb, than it was when it was an A-Bomb or an "invincible" tank — or "Big Bertha" herself. So long as the public feels impotent to change the development of events it will resign itself to its fate, and we applaud its wisdom in refusing to express *preferences* to dying by radiation, roasting or blasting.

Therefore to ensure that we shall not die as a result of nuclear war, it is necessary to abolish war as an inevitable concomitant of our society, as one of the many risks we humans have to accept. If, as we maintain, war is a *means* and not an *end*, then we will never (repeat NEVER) remove the threat of war so long as we continue to accept, or believe in, the hierarchical, class society; or so long as we believe that some are better fitted to run our lives than we are ourselves.

The Campaign for Nuclear Disarmament, as well as those *enfants terribles* of *Tribune* and the Labour "Left" pin all their hopes on legality and the return of the Labour Party at the next elections. What a hope! This week the Shop Workers, one of the Big Six Unions representing more than 300,000 workers voted for the Padley-Crossman compromise defence programme, thereby reversing last year's support of unilateralism. The only argument we could find in their debates and Walter Padley's (one more ex-ILP chairman who has "made the grade") two emotion-laden speeches was the need for unity in the Party. (So much for *Tribune's* boast of the successes of CND's "Patient explanations" winning the TUC for unilateralism). Later in the week the AEU (Amalgamated Engineering Union) reversed its previous support for unilateralism, and so another 800,000 or whatever it is, bloc votes jumped from the pan of unilateralism into the fire of Gaitskellian multilateralism. Poor Michael Foot & Co have surely had the smile wiped off their faces by an ex-ILP'er and the 52-strong National Committee (which includes some 20 *Communists*, whose party anybody who has eyes recognises is now putting its heart and soul into the Collins-Foot unilateral enterprise!).

When, next October, the Labour Conference reverses last year's unilateralist vote in favour of Gaitskell's programme, or even Crossman's Compromise, nothing will have changed. Just as the reversal of the AEU's policy can be explained to a great extent, to quote the *Guardian*, by "clever political management", one can rest assured that whatever government is in power, so long as it enjoys its working majority, neither the voice of reason nor even the outburst of its own fanatics will oblige it to deflect from the path which serves its own personal interests and those of the powers who rule the country.

The only threat to its power and the *status quo* is when enough ordinary people decide to exercise and express their own power, united as equals by a mutual respect which recognises the individuality, the uniqueness of each, a respect which is in contrast with the contempt in which they should hold all politicians and all the servants of State institutions.

The future of the "Committee of 100" is in the *streets* and not the *lobbies*: away from the parties, the personalities and the Parliament Squares, reaching out to the untapped, ignorant perhaps, but generous, masses. And at the same time, developing, hardening the intransigence of the demonstrators themselves. In the process we shall lose a few playwrights and playboys, but what we lost in "names" we will undoubtedly gain in militancy.

(May 13, 1961)

WAR BY ACCIDENT?

A contributor in last week's FREEDOM suggested that the "calmness" of the editorial approach over the Berlin "crisis" was a reaction to the growing "panic", and a feeling that war was inevitable. And he concluded: "Indeed this is an admirable approach, but is it truly honest?" Clearly our friend has not understood our approach. Apart from the fact that we cannot understand how an approach can be admirable and at the same time dishonest, our contention is that we are weakening our anti-war arguments as well as the anarchist case by subscribing to the views that a few leading politicians between them hold the fate of mankind in their hands, or that the possibility of "annihilation by accident" is a reality. It is not that we are afraid of calling a spade a spade but on the contrary it is because it seems to us that if we go on talking about war being imminent, even when it is obvious that it is not, we eventually reach the point where the public is lulled into believing that the politicians will find a way round any particular "crisis", won't believe that a war is on the way when in fact it is imminent.

The pacifists have been talking about the imminence of war and the possibilities of "accidental" wars for at least ten years. We are being told of all the narrow escapes we have had as flocks of birds and other harmless objects have been "mistaken" for the real thing. In our columns this week two correspondents give us a catalogue of the dangers of war by accident. We do not wish to cast doubts on their sources nor their intelligence, but is it not extraordinary, in that case, that war by accident has not occurred a hundred times? Why has the button not been pressed? Our correspondent last week quoted Bertrand Russell as saying that it was "a piece of good luck" upon which it would be imprudent to rely.

We find such arguments most unconvincing. Whilst we cannot confute them with black and white facts since we are not in the confidence of the Establishment, we can draw certain conclusions based on facts. If Bertrand Russell and friends are right, that in the West and presumably in Russia too, there are a handful of individuals whose eyes are glued to radar-type screens and whose index fingers are poised on buttons, the pressing of which will unleash a war of annihilation, *then these men are truly the most powerful individuals in the world today*. We cannot believe that such a state of affairs would be tolerated by the political, military or civil hierarchies in any of these countries. *Coups d'etat*, palace revolutions, would be too easy to stage if one man had more power at his finger tips than a General with a division at his command. And consider the fact that the power of the State depends on the loyalty of the Armed Forces, that is their subordination to the orders of the civil authority, and one does not need much imagination (certainly less than one of our correspondents who repeats the story that in ordering a taxi by short wave radio one might instead launch a missile!) to realise that the button pressers of this nuclear-electronic age when they do, will thereby probably do no more than summon a superior, who in turn will summon his superior and so on. Not only will the power of any individual in the war machine be severely circumscribed for the reasons we have given, but because the element of surprise is absent from modern war — that is a war situation will exist some considerable time before the belligerents actually engage in war — the dangers of "accidental" war are only conceivable when war is in any case imminent; when the professional soldiers are given more power to take spot decisions, and this delegation of power to the men on the spot will obviously be greater in a press button war than in past conflagrations which involved the much slower land forces.

One of our correspondents this week compares our approach with the notorious Macmillan statement, in between rounds of golf, that the "crisis" had been built up by the Press. This comparison was clearly intended to show how reactionary were our arguments*. Is our correspondent maintaining that politicians always tell lies, or that the Press invariably tells the truth? We believe that both will tell the truth when it suits their book and will lie when the truth, or the facts, are not in their interest.

Can anyone doubt that but for the role of mass communications in inventing "crises" or fanning the flames of real but minor crises,

---

* In The Myths of War and Peace (FREEDOM)

the comings and goings, the utterances and the threats of politicians would be largely ignored; wasted breath? But even so, however serious a "crisis" may appear on newsprint, or in the utterances of a leading politician, wars are made of sterner stuff, and certainly not by Fleet Street hacks or the editor of *Pravda*!

In saying this we have never meant to suggest that war is a thing of the past. So long as the affairs of Man are regulated according to concepts based on authority, backed by armed forces, the threat of war will always be with us. And if we wish to abolish war from our lives nothing less than destroying the system and replacing it by a society based on libertarian concepts will do. This is the social revolution — a prospect much less frightening and certainly more positive than cold- or hot-wars, and the sooner we realise that peace and revolution are indivisible the sooner will we know how best to direct our activities against war.

This Sunday the "Committee of 100" will be staging its third mass sit-down in London. FREEDOM has supported, and many anarchists have participated in, these demonstrations, not because we imagined that they would remove the threat of war or that they might influence governments, but because we believe such demonstrations of civil disobedience are important *skirmishes* in the struggle against authority, against the values of existing society and for a new society based on self-responsibility and co-operation. For these reasons we regret the opportunistic approach of the Committee's publicity in connection with this Sunday's sit-down.

> The developing Berlin crisis means that in the next few weeks or months it is quite likely that the buttons will be pushed. War has never been closer or more likely than now.

If our friends of the "Committee of 100" honestly believe the foregoing to be true, then, while respecting their views, we would suggest that they re-examine the facts as well as approach "politics" with a little more healthy cynicism.

> The British authorities have been confronted in the Committee's supporters, by a disarmament movement which has the power to enforce its demands. Their reply has been to ban all meetings in which specific acts of non-violent civil disobedience are advocated.

Do the Committee honestly believe that the "British authorities" are unduly worried or influenced by the sit-downs? If they do, then we can only say that it does not appear to have affected government policies in any way.

The fact that the authorities seek to prevent the Committee from holding its demonstrations *is* important, for it shows only too clearly that the "freedom of speech" to which the government pays lip-service is limited to those bodies which play the "freedom" game according to the rules. But we would suggest that it is in bringing an awareness to its supporters of the limits of freedom in an authoritarian society, and the impotence of the citizen to influence policy in a governmental society, that the importance of the Committee of 100's demonstrations lies.

For not only will the demonstrators be confronted with the negative aspects of government. At the same time they will have to face the positive realities; that freedom is something we must create for ourselves and defend; that the only government over which we have control is self-government. This should lead to new lines of thought.

So long as the government is in power, sit-down demonstrations will leave it unmoved policy wise. But what does upset Governments is that people should not be deterred from breaking the law by the threat of punishments with which the *status quo* is maintained and protected. One can anticipate that if the civil disobedience movement grows, the "law" will be strengthened in an attempt to intimidate the recalcitrants. If these measures fail to break the movement then, it seems to us, the struggle begins in earnest. But in all this, nuclear disarmament will be no more than a minor aspect of the social struggle. Which is as it should be.

(September 16, 1961)

ARE OUR LEADERS SUICIDAL LUNATICS?

Of the long list of possible technical causes of a nuclear war by "accident" by far the most fantastic, to our minds, was the one by which

"a woman calling a taxi in New York on a short circuit wireless sytem, because of the combination of the wavelength of the system and the pitch of her voice, caused a space rocket to be fired at Cape Canavarel".

A new book published in America with the title "The Nation's Safety and Arms Control" gives further "examples" of how a nuclear war could be started by accident. One of the most engaging suggestions is that a squirrel or other rodent nibbling at a cable could send a Minuteman inter-continental missile into the heart of Russia. Replying to this charge, the U.S. Secretary of the Air Force, Mr Eugene Zuckert, points out that there is a complicated system of mechanical and manual controls that will prevent an accidental launching of a Minuteman. He further added that cables used to relay complex, coded communications are buried deep in the ground, that an animal gnawing at a cable will set off an automatic alarm enabling the system to be shut off.

Another charge by Mr Arthur Hadley, the author of the book in question, is that Matador missiles, which can carry a nuclear warhead, are standing unprotected in Europe and can be fired by one man who sleeps beside them. Mr Zuckert replies that "safety controls make it impossible for one man to fire such a missile intentionally or mistakenly".

Of specific "accidents" the book describes an incident in which it is claimed that

two 200-mile range Bomarc missiles automatically erected themselves on their launching pads and were showing exhaust fumes before Air Force officers rushed from a mess hall and pulled wires and threw switches to prevent a launching.

Mr Zuckert says that the only case resembling that took place about a year ago at a U.S. base when two Bomarcs erected themselves because of a short circuit. However, he says, there was no danger of an accidental launching, and denies that smoke came from the exhausts.

Obviously, either Mr Hadley or Mr Zuckert has his facts wrong, and it should not be all that difficult to establish the true facts. In the meantime we can only express opinions, and this writer's is that Mr Zuckert was telling the truth. And the reasons are too many to enumerate here. Perhaps the most obvious is that in spite of the hundreds of possible ways in which it is alleged that missiles could be launched by accident, no such accident has yet occurred. The second most obvious reason is that the technical problems involved in preventing accidental launchings are small compared with those which had to be overcome in developing the weapons and carriers of death, and no self-respecting scientists would overlook such minor details. Why even in our puny day to day domestic arrangements, if a rat gnaws the electric light cable a simple device called a fuse ensures that the house isn't set on fire by the resulting short circuit!

Come, come comrades! Whatever we may think of the level of intelligence of the politicians let us not forget that they are very temporary mouthpieces of a system based on economic privilege and social status for a minority which has successfully defended itself against allcomers, reformers and revolutionaries. To treat this minority as lunatics bent on destroying mankind, themselves included, is to assume, wrongly in our opinion, not only that life means nothing to them, but that their grip on the reins of power in all its aspects is threatened.

It is clear to us that the ruling class is not suicidal and certainly not stupid. It has succeeded in maintaining its privileges by sharing some of its power. It has succeeded in stifling the aspirations of the working class movements by drawing its leaders into the Establishment by the carrot of gadgetry ("A forecast for Europe in 1970" "Washing Machines for all" — *Guardian*, October 30), and by its stranglehold on mass communications media. It has introduced a permanent cold-war economy which serves both as an effective financial cushion for the crises of capitalism as well as a psychological weapon against social change.

No mere change of government can or will alter the existing structure of society. Are we not witnessing this truth throughout the African continent where a new propertied class is emerging as the white "colons" sell out; where a new group of politicians simply takes over where their white predecessors left off. (Indeed to ensure the continuity of the system many white officials are retained as advisers.)

All this makes resistance and revolution more necessary than ever, and not, as many think, outmoded. For if nothing else is clear in the world we live in, one fact is crystal clear: that the ruling classes throughout the world are consolidating and not abdicating their power. And if the people want peace (and the only guarantee is a completely disarmed world), justice (so long as there is privilege there can be no justice) and freedom (so long as some men have the power to direct the lives of other men there can be no freedom) they must destroy the present power structure of society.

Sitting-down and allowing oneself to be carried off to gaol is proving an effective propaganda weapon, and most important of all is probably making some of those who join in these demonstrations think along unorthodox, revolutionary lines. In this sense it contains the germs of a revolutionary movement of the people. "Banning the Bomb" is a slogan acceptable by the respectable as well as the revolutionary, but it is a fact that on most other aspects of the social problems from which war stems, the demonstrators are divided. Only a few see in civil disobedience a first step in a revolutionary struggle against the power of the State, which allows government and ruling class to ignore them so far as their actions and policies are concerned.

Many involved in the activities of the Committee of 100 are aware of this and it is encouraging to see that much discussion and rethinking are going on. What is less encouraging are indications that the so-called "New Left" is making a bid to impress its rigid political formulae on the movement. This can only have disastrous consequences if allowed to continue unchallenged. It seems to us that anarchists and other libertarians have an important part to play in the free development of this, at present, spontaneous protest movement of youth.

(November 4, 1961)

LEADERS AND LUNATICS

Arthur Uloth's "complete disagreement" with our approach would seem to us to hinge on only one question. We agree that it is an important one, but nevertheless one on which reasonable people should be able to reach agreement because it is a question of facts and not opinion or conjecture. The question is contained in the last two sentences of his first paragraph:

> People in all walks of life commit suicide and occasionally murder. The danger comes when one of these unbalanced people comes to hold a position of supreme power.

He illustrates his contention in the second paragraph with the examples of Stalin and Hitler "as well as some of the Roman emperors". Perhaps we should forget about the Roman emperors "and other rulers in different periods of history" for the time being, and content ourselves with events and leaders in our own times.

Who are the individuals, suicidal, murderous or just "unbalanced" who have *in fact* held positions of *supreme power*? Before we start thinking of the likely candidates, let us attempt to define "supreme power". As we understand it, and we are naturally open to correction, it is the absolute power which an individual enjoys to direct the lives, the action, the thoughts, of all the members of the community by reason of wisdom, hypnotic powers, or the exclusive possession of a weapon of coercion (it could be as fantastic as a portable "death ray" or as pedestrian as an age-long taboo). In other words we maintain that for an *individual* to enjoy supreme power he must embody in his person not only the desire, the ambition, or the God-sent-mission, to direct, control or guide the lives of all other members of the community, but also the *power* to enforce his wishes upon those who might not recognise either his wisdom or his authority. Among the latter are, on the one hand, the Arthur Uloths and the writer of these lines, who neither want to rule nor be ruled, and on the other, those who are as avid for positions of power as our would-be "supreme ruler".

If we overlook for the time being the Uloths and this writer we are left with a very large number of people all interested in maintaining, consolidating or achieving positions of privilege which are, and can only be, based on power over their lives of other people.

Willy nilly we are born into a class-divided world, in which for some of us the red carpet of social and economic privilege is laid down even before our contemplated arrival. But for most of us our often unexpected arrival is preceded by overtime at work, housing problems, a tightening-of-the-belt, and our chequered future is determined by the family fortunes and the imponderables of 11-plus examinations, to mention only two of the obstacles barring the way to most children. (Agreed that the children of the privileged class are as much the victims of *their* environment as the children of the have-nots are of theirs. But . . . !)

This is not a digression but an attempt to draw attention to the fact that the underprivileged majority find themselves in the position they are in, *not* because they are less intelligent nor potentially less able to occupy more "responsible" jobs than the privileged minority, but because of the accident of birth and the very palpable fact that the society into which they are born has for a very long time been geared to satisfying primarily the demands and aspirations of the privileged. And such a society depends for its existence on the needs of the majority being subordinated to those of a minority. (Let us hasten to add that, we anarchists are as unconvinced by rule of the majority as we are of rule by the minority, since we mistrust the intentions of those who desire to rule just as, in despair, we question the intelligence of those who accept to be ruled.)

Now, how does a minority manage to retain its power in the teeth of a dissatisfied — to say the least — majority? The unsubtle, brutal answer is: *force*. Call it the threat of —, call it law-and-order, call it the fear of unemployment or "insecurity"; blame the Joneses, "tradition", "human nature", "survival of the fittest", the wickedness of man" or "man's aggressivity"; indeed, call it by any name you like but you cannot escape from the fact that a minority rules over the majority because it disposes of the machinery of State, that is, the armed forces, the Civil Service, the police, the judiciary, the prisons, mass communications, the means of production as well as the raw materials below and above ground. In a word, *they* hold all the cards of power except the aces which are held by the people, the majority, who are the *producers* of the means of life (and the luxuries of the privileged minority), but who have still to discover what they have up their sleeves.

The privileged minority are the victims of their own greed. Apart from the very important fact that in usurping culture, knowledge and education they spawned the most determined rebels within their own class, the growth of industrialism, by which larger profits could be made than by the cultivation of the land, has not only extended the horizons and the frontiers of the privileged minority but also their dependence on a new class of technicians, scientists, financiers and super-salesmen undreamed of a century ago.

The "supreme power" of an individual, which Arthur Uloth refers to, which is in fact absolute power, is a thing of the past. Whereas in the distant past the absolute monarch secured his power by granting sinecures and property to loyal soldiers and financial backers, today it is the other way round. The monarchy — where it still persists it is no more than an expensive, dormant, appendix in the social organism — and governments, are the vocal stooges of the industrialists, the financiers and the permanent civil servants who between them seek to regulate our lives. Not only has the number of aspirants to "supreme power" increased as taboos have been broken down, but so has *their* dependence on others increased in order to maintain what power they have.

To our minds those who today wield the least power in the Western bloc are the politicians. (Let us qualify this by saying that if the governments of the West European and American bloc have real power of decision it is only because their spokesmen are themselves influential members of the ruling élite in their respective countries. Fact or fiction?) In the Russian bloc, though the financier and industrialist as we understand them in the West, do not exist, effective power must (unless one believes that everything from a sputnik to a shoe-lace can be ordered and controlled from Khrushchev's office in Moscow) be widely spread amongst scientists, technicians, bureaucrats, soldiers, policemen and politicians. When Mr K at the recent Soviet Party Congress declared that the very speech he was then making had been "examined and endorsed by the leading collective" he was being more honest, more realistic as to the *powers* of the political leaders than for instance such impotent political nincompoops as our Lord Home who, perhaps because he was at the time of his appointment widely described as a Macmillan stooge, now cannot make a speech without threatening Her Majesty's potential enemies with an H-Bomb (made in Britain) right in their vital spot.

One of our tasks is to expose the hypocrisy of the political game of creating political crises, of "negotiating", patching-up, postponing, but never solving or eradicating them. Our task is to *deflate* these newspaper-personalities, not to *inflate* them, which, unwittingly, our friend Uloth does when he suggests they might well hold positions of "supreme power". Just think of the awe in which people such as Hitler, Stalin, Roosevelt and Churchill were held *by the organs of mass communications*, and in consequence by the masses. They are all dead, politically if not physically, and at the time of writing Adenauer, Khrushchev, Kennedy and Macmillan are the "personalities" that have replaced them.

Firstly not only have the countries concerned survived the loss of their super-men; they all boast that they have never been as prosperous as they are now . . . without them! Secondly, with the possible exception of Britain (which apparently still talks of the greatness of Churchill in spite of the valid denunciations by his critical civil and military "colleagues"), the Stalins, Roosevelts and Hitlers (not to mention Mussolinis) get the criticism or oblivion they deserve. Why? Not because they were mad, as Arthur Uloth suggests, but because they have been used as the scapegoats for the real "powers behind the throne" and because once the spotlight of mass communications has been turned elsewhere they assume their normal stature, and the world can only see them as vain, weak, ambitious, lonely, ruthless, unbalanced, stupid, or whatever human beings can be in given circumstances. But are we asked to accept that the worker in Russia, in Italy, in Germany, America, France and Britain is now any less a worker, a member of the *other class*, than he was when the other set of supermen were in office? If not then these self-professed champions of the people are no more the defenders of the people than their much denounced predecessors.

"Of course the social system has not changed", declares Arthur Uloth, adding, "And no doubt revolution is the only answer". We agree 100 per cent! And when he writes

But we should be living in a fool's paradise if we imagine that 'it can't happen'. As long as these weapons of mass destruction exist there is always a risk that they may be used, or set off by an error of judgment that cannot be corrected in time

we are again in agreement. We have never said that "it can't happen". Indeed, if he had read our last editorial in conjunction with the others we have written on the subject he would have found in the opening sentence of *The Myth of War and Peace* (September 2) the following:

In the kind of world set-up which regulates human affairs the possibility of war at some time or other is inevitable . . .

And far from assuming that "accidental" war could result from a technical hitch we have sought to pour cold water on these fantastic "stories". But neither do we believe that war will be the result of what comrade Uloth calls "the obvious fact of human irrationality". Wars are launched by the ruling class for reasons which are, for them, very rational: their survival as a privileged class. Our argument is that for them to take such a step they must feel that their security is threatened. In spite of Mr K and the Committee of 100 (to whom, in spite of what some of our critics may say, we have offered all along 100 per cent support so long as they don't sell-out to the Establishment or "New" Left politicians) we do not consider that they are, or feel, so threatened and for these reasons we see no missiles on the launching pads just waiting for the unknown "criminal" to press the button that will start the fireworks and the deadly blast and fall-out.

Arthur Uloth will, we hope, permit us to underline his concluding point that the weapons of mass destruction "may be used, or set off by an error of judgment that cannot be corrected in time". All wars are an error of judgment so far as the losing side is concerned and viewed in retrospect, but there is a chasm of irrationality between the argument that we are threatened by suicidal lunatics "in positions of supreme power" and that wars are the result of "an error of judgment".

Would that the ruling groups were lunatics; one would know how to deal with them. They are not lunatics but people who, as the saying goes, know on which side their bread is buttered, and have their finger on the pulse of public opinion, market trends, Common Markets and subversive activities.* Only too well do the ruling class know what they want. It's the working people who serve their interests who still don't know what *they* want.

(November 11, 1961)

---

* Mr Bruce Reid, Press Officer of the Committee of 100 stated, according to the *Sunday Times* that the Special Branch of Scotland Yard was paying special attention to their activities on Home Office instructions. "The Police were very much in evidence at meetings we held at the docks". We would add that at the Committee's Trafalgar Square meeting on October 29 this writer saw a group of four plain clothes men all wearing CND badges mingling with the crowd.

SOLIDARITY WANTED FOR SCHOENMAN AND CLARK

In theory Ralph Schoenman, the American student who last Friday completed a two months' sentence in one of Her Majesty's prisons for "inciting the public to commit breaches of the peace", (to wit, to take part in the sit-down demonstration at Trafalgar Square on September 17), should have left our shores by the time these lines are printed. His permit expired and the Home Secretary will not renew it. This is a polite and hypocritical way of saying that he is to be deported as an undesirable alien. Of course Mr Butler, the Home Secretary, who likes to be considered an enlightened Tory, wants to be fair. In a letter to Fenner Brockway he writes: "I realise of course that he will want a short time after he leaves prison to put his affairs in order and I shall not seek to enforce his departure before the end of the month".

In theory George Clark sentenced at the same time as Ralph Schoenman was due to be released on the same day. But two days earlier, he was taken from prison to appear at London Sessions in connection with an earlier demonstration which took place outside the American Embassy on September 6th. He was sentenced to a further *nine months* for having organised a sit-down and for refusing to undertake to keep the peace. Since the technical obstruction caused by sitting down carries a maximum penalty of a £2 fine it means that the nine months sentence was the punishment imposed by the chairman, Mr R.E. Seaton, for George Clark's refusal to be bound over to keep the peace.

The savagery of the sentence, the more so since it follows on a two months sentence imposed for a similar refusal on September 13 (that is even before the demonstration of September 17 took place), has not awakened the consciences of our liberal Press. Yet in the deportation of Ralph Schoenman and the sadistic, cat-and-mouse treatment of George Clark the State has clearly shown *the slender limits of its tolerance and patience for the dissenters in our midst*. We italicise those words of the last sentence not because we are surprised or shocked by developments, but in order to underline a point we anarchists have been making all along, and which seems to have escaped the notice of those more "trusting" demonstrators who honestly, but naively, if we may say so, believe that governments — by which they mean the ruling class — are open to persuasion by the people, when they take the trouble to publicly express their deeply-felt concern for the future of mankind.

The attitude of government to interference in its legally sanctioned mission(!) of governing is best summed up in the remarks by the chairman at London Sessions when George Clark refused to give "an undertaking to keep the peace".

> We all have to live in the world as it is today and from what you have said, your efforts have done nothing to improve it. You are a nuisance to the overworked and understaffed police and will have to go to prison for nine months.

(Can we presume from the foregoing that if the police were neither overworked nor understaffed he would not have been such a nuisance and would therefore have received a lighter sentence?)

And when members of the public in the court received the sentence with "loud cries of 'shame' ", Mr Seaton commented: "If there is any more of this, there will be more of you going inside".

This latter remark shows that the Chairman of London Sessions is not a fit person to sit in judgment over others since clearly he can neither control his emotions nor hide the corroding effect that occupying even his modest seat of power has had on him.

Now, the Committee of 100 are loathe on principle (or is it for tactical reasons?) to protest or take any kind of action either in the exceptional circumstances of Ralph Schoenman — an alien in the eyes of the law, albeit the citizen of a nation which could be described as our closest nuclear friend — or in such more everyday matters as police behaviour at demonstrations, and gross abuses by magistrates and judges so far as sentences imposed as well as in the gratuitous remarks they make in their courts, is concerned. Perhaps because we do not believe that martyrdom is the passport to a better world, though we recognise that persecution is a price that all serious reformers and revolutionaries must expect to pay for their militancy, we should not hesitate to demand that neither the police nor the courts should abuse their powers. Are they not all-embracing enough for us not to allow them to abuse them as well without protest?

To allow Ralph Schoenman to be deported, and George Clark to be subjected to a cat-and-mouse treatment without protest and agitation is to acquiesce in the mockery of democracy. The government professes to believe in democracy. If we do not believe its protestations let us not miss one occasion to challenge it, or to expose it to ridicule when it stubbornly refuses to give way on minor issues such as are in fact the cases of our two friends.

For us these are not minor issues. Ralph Schoenman and George Clark are victims of political persecution. On what grounds other than *political* does the Home Secretary refuse to renew the former's permit to remain in this country? And in the case of George Clark the savage sentence imposed on him by the Chairman of London Sessions was not only a sop to the police but a warning to those who take part in future demonstrations of what they might expect if they are picked up. What have these considerations to do with making the punishment of George Clark fit his crime?

Well, then, what are we going to do? Sit back and wallow in our self-righteous impotence or protest publicly, loudly, forcibly, even if in the end we fail. Here is an issue where pacifists, anarchists, social creditors, freethinkers, Tribunites, liberals, Welsh Nationalists and others could unite in a common effort and a common cause without losing their identity. The aim: to reverse the deportation order on Ralph Schoenman and to quash the sentence on George Clark. And if we succeed we will have shown a little human solidarity; if we fail, we will at least have done all in our power for two worthy members of the human family.

(November 18, 1961)

WETHERSFIELD SIT-DOWN

At Finchingfield, where the CND's Easter march assembled and spilled over into the innumerable roads and lanes that meet there, the village green was deserted. Still we were not expecting to see demonstrators assembled there, though we were hoping that, in view of the last minute refusal by the coach people to take people from London we would meet isolated groups on the road leading to Wethersfield. Wethersfield village contrasted sharply with sleepy Finchingfield. The Press were there in strength; the cameras mounted on car roofs, rubber cables connected to black boxes, and men with ear-phones; men with more cameras strapped to their bodies than they had hands to handle them; and of course the Force, the custodians of law and order were there in strength. They were lining the streets like sinister festoons for a village in mourning; the village hall was bursting its sides with the Reserves, kept warm with hot refreshments and food. After all, like the Americans at the base they were, to quote the Minister, "the guests" of Wethersfield. The Press were there, the police were there, and the alsatians were there, barking away in the vans. But alas, enough demonstrators were not there for the show to start, for the wheels to turn; for the forces of law and order to put away their pipes and stub out their cigarettes and put on their masks; for the news gatherers to take up their action stations.

Hopefully we went on to Braintree to offer transport for stranded demonstrators. At the station there were more signs of life, but even so it was clear that no more than a token demonstration would be possible. Shortly after 1.30 all the transport moved off, plain clothes men and news men as well as demonstrators, on the road to Wethersfield.

The demonstrators assembled in two columns, 500 of them in all. Of these only about 100 were prepared to attempt to penetrate the barbed wire defences and since the organisers had felt that a minimum of 500 were needed for this "operation" alone, it was decided that all available demonstrators should be used to block the two entrances to the air base. So off we marched with our escorts along the winding road that led to the base. Once there, we were faced with a double line of police and most of our group of about 250 sat down. It was then 3 pm. About a quarter of an hour later three organisers from the front of the group were picked up and taken away in a van. Shortly afterwards two military ambulances with bells ringing and the red cross lighted up arrived and stopped. What should we do; there were those who said "sit down" and others who thought we should get up; there was the rosy cheeked girl on the side lines who cried out, "Don't get up; they played the same trick at Croydon". And of course we were not to know that at the other gate they were playing just the same mean trick. To our minds we were right to get up and give them the benefit of the doubt. Ambulances are the symbol of man's humanity to man, and it is surely the aim of demonstrators to foster such a spirit. That the authorities use ambulances for other purposes in time of peace as well as in war, can only underline the baseness of those against whom the people's struggle has to be directed.

To keep the demonstrators on the *qui vive* another five were picked up and taken away about an hour later. Darkness descended, the police on duty were periodically relieved, the figures lining the fences became silhouettes, the two helicopters which like noisy dachshunds had been enjoying themselves hovering overhead blowing hats off and showing off their power to squash us like ants underfoot, retired for tea or coca cola. A few servicemen hurled their abuse across the darkened fields and one of our number, a strong-voiced youngster, hurled her healthy epithets back into the darkness, while a few of our number tut-tutted that we didn't do that kind of thing.

Six pm and we were still there; just changing of the guard with some of them taking the muddy route on the edge of the field, others instead finding it more fun to push and kick their ways through the small field of squatters. At 6.30 pm only half an hour before the demonstration was due to end, a van arrived and an inspector followed by his posse of coppers made his way into the assembly shining his big torch into faces and, presumably guided by a man's face, would bark out to his followers "take him away" or "this one" and they would pounce on the victim and take him off, and since the operation took place only in the light of a couple of torches, those in the vicinity of the victim were trampled on, had knees poked into their backs, not intentionally of course! And in this way some twenty more demonstrators were whisked off to the police-station. This little operation reminded one of a scene we had witnessed in a farmyard years ago where the farmer when he wanted a chicken for lunch would first survey his flock and when he spotted the one he fancied for the pot would point it out and his faithful dog, always by his side, would simply rush into the flock and grab the victim by its neck, and, tail wagging, bring it to his master, alive, a little sore in the neck probably — but then if the chicken could have realised that its neck was due to be broken, it would have appreciated the delicacy with which the dog had done its job.

The operation stirred up discussion, as we all huddled a little closer together to close the gaps as well as to try and keep warm, with some demonstrators declaring that we should continue to sit after 7 pm in view of the latest provocation. But most of us felt that no purpose would be served by this. The point was still being debated ten minutes little when an insignificant little Ford car with just the driver was brought onto the scene. Obviously some very important person, perhaps the Minister in disguise. "Make way for this car", came the orders from the Inspectors who with two lines of policemen escorted this miserable little motor. Nobody moved, and the forces of law and order went into action. Dragging, picking up and throwing people into the muddy ploughed field. Some returned and placed themselves in the path of the car and were hurled back. Now here was a case of obstructing the police, yet not a single demonstrator was arrested. A quarter of an hour earlier, twenty had been arrested for no apparent reason!'

At 7 pm a muddy column of 200 wound its way along the country lanes back to Wethersfield. Behind us, lighting the way, were the motorised forces of law and order driving at *pas d'homme*. The day's sport — it was cat and mouse — was over. The column broke up in the village, the line of motor-cycles, police cars, police vans and plain vans with barking dogs passed us, the dogs back to their kennels, the policemen back to theirs, and we adjourned to discuss the day's events and gather what news we could of Ruislip, Bristol, Manchester, York and Brize Norton.

(December 16, 1961)

INQUEST ON THE SIT-DOWN — I

How should we go about the question of assessing last Saturday's sit-down and other demonstrations organised by the Committee of 100 and its regional counterparts? By the total number of supporters who attended? By the number of arrests, by the numbers who refused to give their names or be bound over? By the numbers jailed, by the reactions of the Press as well as the publicity received? To our minds, these are poor yardsticks at this stage in the development of the loose movement which supports the activities of the Committee, by which to assess such demonstrations, and those of us who take part must be the first to insist that the Committee should not be tempted to encourage the assessment of the success or failure of any demonstration by a counting of heads, of arrests, of people kicking their heels in jail.

Even from the point of view of publicity, it is a mistake for it is just what the Press revels in, and when the "numbers" do not reach the estimates they can, with some justification, overlook other aspects of a demonstration which may have been highly successful, and write it off as a failure because the "numbers" were below the organisers' expectations. Apart from the *Observer* whose headline "6000 disarmers' gesture ends in 850 arrests" was as admirable as its sour little editorial comment was typical, the other papers exploited "numbers" — success and failure. Thus the *Sunday Pictorial's* "ARRESTS BY THE HUNDRED — as A-base invasion flops", the *Sunday Times'* "850 ARRESTS BUT ANTI-BOMB DAY FIZZLES OUT", the *News of the World's* "The great bomb protest is a damp squib. HUNDREDS HELD" and the *Sunday Telegraph's* "Flop-down fizzle in the fog". Of course the Press insists on having it all ways. Before the demonstrations take place they deprecate the actions the Committee and its supporters propose to engage in; when, in the event, they fail to do what they proposed to do, then the Press sneers at their failure, forgetting that their original concern in deprecating the action was that the national safety was being threatened!

From this stems a further point which should be given serious consideration: does the "movement" still need to hold demonstrations which are clearly intended to appeal to what the Press calls "news", and therefore to receive maximum publicity which is a mixture of good and bad? It seems to us that there were strong grounds for such considerations in the early days of the "movement" since money and the instruments of mass communications are in the hands of the upholders of the Establishment, and it was legitimate to appeal to others to join one in activities in which one courted arrest and imprisonment, as an example to others, as well as a means of "hitting the headlines".

There can be no doubt whatever as to the importance of the activities of the original Direct Action Committee in shaking off some of the apathy, the hopeless fatalism and defeatism which had enshrouded the more or less progressive, thinking, elements in this country (a situation probably contributed to by the inability of the Labour Party to win even a general election). But it seems to us that the kind of *useful* publicity that the National Press could be expected to give to the activities of the Committee of 100 is now exhausted. We would certainly not advise anybody to accept a prison sentence resulting from a civil disobedience demonstration for the publicity it might be expected to receive, and by implication, the influence it might have on the public. We must qualify this statement in order to express our true feelings and views.

The Press and mass communications are interested in "personalities" and not in individuals. *They* create the "personalities"; *you* establish your individuality. Now, if you decide to earn your living in the show business, in politics or in any occupation in which you need to be recognised by the mass public as somebody outside the run of ordinary human beings, you seek the aid of the Press, TV, and ITV, or better still you employ an agent who is on paying and drinking terms with the "blokes that matter" in mass communications. They build your "public personality" and destroy your individuality.

For the "personalities", so long as it doesn't keep them out of the public eye too long or disrupt their contracts, involvement in sit-downs is good publicity for them and, incidentally, for the "cause" (though the value is dubious since while on the one hand it tends to encourage the waverers, on the other it bestows a halo of responsibility on a movement which has no intention of being "respectable").

But for the likes of you and the writer of these lines the publicity value of going to prison as the alternative to paying a fine or agreeing to be bound over has very little chance of making the headlines of the mass Press or of influencing its readers if it did. The decision to (*a*) participate in demonstrations involving the risk of arrest, (*b*) refuse to pay fines and accept imprisonment, (*c*) accept committal to prison as the price for refusing to be "bound over" to keep the peace must be a personal one, by which we mean a responsible one, shorn of heroics, fanaticism, emotionalism, spleen, exhibitionism and defiance. We accept any of these feelings as explanations for one's actions on *one* occasion; they are a kind of liberation for a whole series of pent-up feelings and fears and doubts which apply especially to young and inexperienced people (and we counsel them as salutary antidotes to the ravages of age, comfort, prosperity, routine and despair which afflict too many of our middle-aged contemporaries). But surely once is enough to liberate us from the inexperience or to shake off the cobwebs of age; to go on meekly offering our necks to the executioners is to deserve what we get. Let us enlarge on the points on which we feel every individual must decide.

The decision to participate in demonstrations involving the risk of arrest. Perhaps, if we deal with a real experience and not with the problem in the abstract, the point we are trying to make will receive from our active readers and the militants of the Committee of 100 the consideration we are bold enough to think it deserves.

This writer has all along supported the initiatives taken by the Committee of 100, without sharing their faith and hopes in a non-violent social revolution and firmly disassociating himself from the muddled political thinking of their chairman, Bertrand Russell, whom we deeply respect and admire as a human being, nevertheless. We have supported them because we felt that they had realised that in order to save mankind from possible annihilation by the latest in the weapons of extermination it was the people, and not governments or political parties, who should be prevailed upon to take action to remove the threat of war. And the sit-down demonstrations they organised besides the country- and world-wide publicity they received, served to break down the blind acceptance with which the majority of people swallowed the orders and policies of the party in office. They also served to remove the social fears of being "involved with the law". The policeman ceased to be for them the "bobby" and assumed his true role as the ruling class's strongest argument. Prison was a place to which social as well as anti-social members of the community might well be sent in the name of law and order. Prison is a place where young and not so young can discover and re-discover their dignity and power as individual human beings despite the fact that within those walls they officially have no rights, no power.

For the militant, the activist, prison should hold no fears. But it is, whatever use one can make of the enforced leisure to read and study, to develop one's individuality, and influence-by-example one's circle of friends, a serious restriction on one's freedom of movement and of communication, to mention the most obvious, and one that we anarchists, at least, do not accept without first asking ourselves whether the price we may have to pay for our actions is worthwhile.

We must always be reluctant to go to prison, which does not mean we should be reluctant to take actions which might involve us in arrest and imprisonment. We should be prepared to court imprisonment if by doing so we further our cause more effectively than we could otherwise, but we must be careful to distinguish between such action and that action which is intended to solve purely personal problems. We know that there will be those who argue that these are one and the self same thing. The fact is that for some of us they are not, and therefore reasonable people must agree to disagree.

This writer had intended to join the Wethersfield demonstration as an observer, partly because the plan to immobilise the air base seemed hopeless at this stage and the price for failure much too high. When we saw how few were those who had made their way to Wethersfield and that the attempt to penetrate the barbed wire fences of the air base (protected by some 3,000 military and civilian police, not to mention the dogs and as we learned, on the spot, helicopters as well) had been called off, a feeling of solidarity with those who had kept the *rendezvous*, and in particular a regard for close friends deeply committed to the demonstration, outweighed our reason — and we sat down with them.

Happy as we are thinking back on one more experience of warm, human companionship, the sharing with others of a cup of hot soup, or the relative protection of a sack between wet macadam and bottom, we are filled with doubts as to whether we were right in joining the sit-down, especially if our action influenced our friends. (If this is boastful thinking we can only reply that in the event our friends influenced us more than we influenced them. But we must add that their influence was emotional.) This is not the way to carry on the struggle against the forces of authority. Demonstrations which involve the possibility of arrest, police violence, and imprisonment must not be treated lightly, as a weekend outing.

Because we consider them as serious non-violent threats to authority, we felt that the Committee of 100 when they originally stated that their acts of civil disobedience would take place only if a minimum of 2,000 people pledged themselves to take part, clearly valued the person of the demonstrator as highly as his "witness". A demonstration of 2,000 had the possibility of success so far as limited objectives were concerned, or failing that, ensured either immunity from arrest or mass arrests which would cause a breakdown of the Court machinery and of the prisons if demonstrators refused to pay fines. This was a reasonable supposition perhaps a year ago. (Strange as it may seem to those who look upon the ruling class as stupid and suicidal, they seem to recognise the danger signals more clearly than their enemies.) Knowing that there was a reception committee of the Establishment of some

3,000 military and civilian police at Wethersfield, that the coach company had refused transport facilities, the Committee of 100 should, at its eve of the demonstration briefing, have held a secret meeting with its Wetherfield marshals calling-off that demonstration and asking them to intercept would-be demonstrators at the London Station and on the highways and suggest they join the Ruislip demonstration.

Instead of which the 500 demonstrators who made their way to Wethersfield were faced with overwhelming odds even before they set off for the two entrances to the base. In the village itself one felt as if in a trap, what with the police and all the paraphernalia of the Press, and this writer and others were convinced that it would have been more effective if all this machine had been set in motion, the barbed wire reinforcements set up, the guards posted at every two yards round the perimeter, the 800 police brought from all over Essex, the dogs, the Randolph Churchills, the Minister, the lot and no demonstrators rather than two columns of 250 people with whom the police played as a cat does with a mouse. To subject demonstrators to such treatment is bad for morale and will harm future activities of the Committee. We only hope that before embarking upon another demonstration these and other important matters will be carefully considered by them.

(December 16, 1961)

II. MUST WE FILL THE PRISONS?

Kingsley Martin in an article on the *Outlook for CND* (*New Statesman*, December 15) discusses at some length the composition of the movement around the Committee of 100.

In view of official Labour's hostility, many active young members of the CND, who were already complaining that its progress was too slow, readily responded to the spectacular tactics of the Committee of 100. Broadly its members fell into three categories. First it includes many CND members who have been converted to civil disobedience. A large proportion of them are still members of the Labour Party. Secondly, there is a sizeable body of non-political enthusiasts who are inspired with a horror of nuclear war but not at all clear where they are going. (Some of them are attracted to the Liberal Party.) But the dangerous truth is — and it had better be stated — that such people might fall a prey to any well-conceived propaganda. Thirdly, there is a small group, prominent amongst the leaders, who are avowedly 'anarchists' in the sense that they believe all politics are hopelessly corrupt and futile, and that in this apocalyptic age the only hope is to end what they regard as a pretence of democracy. They are ready to challenge existing governments by any non-violent means. Philosophically they stand at the opposite pole from the Communists, who are a negligible fraction.

Some of this anarchist group seriously argue that if the 1,300 arrests in Trafalgar Square and the 850 arrested last week-end can be increased to 30,000 or 50,000 in future week-ends, the governments of Britain could not imprison them all and would have to throw up the sponge. What exactly is to happen then is not clear.

To this perceptive analysis he draws an equally perceptive, but to our minds, unduly pessimistic conclusion that

To most of us such an attitude appears a sad example of 'infantile leftism' — which is the quickest route to Fascism. This, however, is unlikely to be the upshot, since the mass of sitters will have turned their attention to other methods long before England is confronted with any such breakdown of government. The kingdom of England is no more likely to be taken by storm than the kingdom of God. Supporters of the Committee of 100 may begin to wonder whether they have achieved anything except publicity. Have they prematurely abandoned more normal methods of propaganda?

The pessimistic note in these conclusions (which is followed by proposals that CND should continue to seek its support within the Labour Party) is indicative of a hardening of the arteries. Though we do not share his "faith" in the . . . infallibility of the "kingdom of England" we agree that it is made of much sterner stuff than some enthusiasts among the sit-downers would seem to believe. And if they are not to suffer the fate of Kingsley Martin, now is the time for a serious appraisal of the achievements and failures, the potentialities as well as the realities confronting this virile movement of revolt.

"Supporters of the Committee of 100 may begin to wonder whether they have achieved anything except publicity". Surely publicity has been the *raison d'etre* of the Committee's demonstrations and in this respect they have been eminently successful. However hostile the Press has shown itself editorially, and however distorted its reports have been, it has been unable to ignore the demonstrations (incidentally, *Tribune* published no report on the seven demonstrations that took place on December 9th). And from one's personal contacts with the uncommitted general public it is clear that very few people in this country are unaware of the existence of the sit-down movement and that *many, many* people have been deeply affected, have been provoked into thinking a little for themselves by the demonstrations and by what Mr Martin calls "the spectacular tactics" of the Committee of 100.

But, in our opinion, it is now time to consolidate what has been achieved in one year's activity. And though the activity we propose is less spectacular than demonstrations of civil disobedience, it also confronts one with problems and decisions which are more long term, and therefore imply a deeper involvement and commitment, than sporadic, symbolic, emotional actions against Authority. It is significant that today there are many thousands of people in this country willing to participate in "illegal" demonstrations at which they court arrest and imprisonment for their actions, yet at the same time the "crisis of our time" is that the progressive minority movements are crippled by a dearth of propagandists to spread ideas, to incite thought and action among their fellow beings. Drawing attention to this phenomenon neither puts us in the CND camp nor makes us into supporters of Kingsley Martin. We oppose both, not because they advocate propaganda by legal methods, but because they seek to perpetuate the illusion that revolutionary changes in the structure of the State can be achieved without destroying the State itself.

Our "criticism" of the Committee of 100 is that, so far, they have tended to foster the illusion that the violence of our existing social system can be destroyed by massive non-violent demonstrations, of civil disobedience, legally — that is, openly — organised. We consider this to be a naive, utopian approach, and would agree with Kingsley Martin's criticisms if he had not suggested that he was criticising the "anarchist group's" argument, which it is not, at least, so far as this writer is concerned.

What do we anarchists believe in fact? Because we believe that human beings can achieve their maximum development and fulfilment as individuals in a community of individuals only when they have free access to the means of life and are equals among equals, we maintain that to achieve a society in which these conditions are possible it is necessary to destroy all that is authoritarian in existing society. But if we are to persuade as many of our fellow beings as possible as to the rightness of the need to destroy, we must also convince them that the reorganisation of the social and economic life of the community along libertarian lines is possible as well as desirable.

Therefore, as we see it, the achievement of the free society (by which we mean the society in which discussion and not violence will regulate human relations) can only be achieved by a series of steps, by each of which the power of government and the privileged class will be weakened as the people take over direct control of certain aspects of their daily lives. This is not to be confused with the reformism of the, often well-meaning, Lib-Labs who do no more than seek to secure concessions for the many in order to persuade them to accept to live in a society designed to serve the privileged few. The steps to anarchy which we advocate, aim at freeing the many from dependence on initiative coming from the State, by making them aware of the simple fact that whatever initiative the State takes on their behalf could be equally, if not better, done by the people themselves. It is a fact that every service we receive "as of right" we actually provide by our labour. In withdrawing the initiative from the State not only do we strengthen initiative and sense of responsibility among the people. We also consolidate resistance and hostility to the State.

We also believe, unlike the social democrats and their "solid majorities", that radical changes in society are always brought about by minorities who know what they want, who not only believe that what they want is good for them (and will not curtail the freedom of their fellow beings), but are prepared to struggle and make "sacrifices" to achieve their ends. For this reason while agreeing with much of last week's *Peace News* editorial on "December 9" we profoundly disagree with their view that

> If we want a genuine policy of disarmament to be implemented then it is idiotic to expect this without the support and consent of most people in this country.

Indeed, we wonder whether even *they* agree, for earlier in the same paragraph our pacifist friends write

> If we believe in the need for mass non-violent action to curb governments from launching war, then we have to win over the people who will go on strike, who will refuse to make nuclear weapons or to man bases, and will sit down with us.

The strike weapon is surely a glaring example of the ability of a minority of the community to paralyse government and the "will of the people" (if it could be ascertained, for instance, that the majority of the people had been bamboozled into believing that they preferred annihilation to say, "red dictatorship"). *We* believe in the strike weapon because in spite of what the capitalist Press says about a handful of workers "holding the country to ransom" it is clear that *only in a capitalist society* with its particular forms of centralised organisation, and dependence on force and the weapons of force to implement its policies, could a strike of even a relatively small number of key workers threaten its authority. But no such strike could, in fact, hold the *country* to ransom. For when it comes to the point man *can* live by bread and water alone! And to provide these most housewives could, in the circumstances, fill the gap more than adequately.

We were saying that we did not believe in the "solid majority" acting in the direction of change for the good — any more than we believe that an "enlightened" elite, armed to the teeth with the weapons of physical and mental coercion, might legislate for the kind of society which we think will bring out the best in all of us. What we do believe is that when a large enough minority of the people who know what they want, who love their fellow beings enough not to want something which they could only achieve at their expense, and who value what they want from life more than the "comfort" and gadgetry which high pressure salesmanship tries to make them believe are the necessities of life in the sixties (How right old Thoreau was when more than a century ago he wrote: "Every generation laughs at the old fashions, but religiously follows the new"), then a step in the right direction is possible. The solid majority, as Malatesta and other anarchists were pointing out even in the heyday of socialism, are reactionary, conservative, and understandably so. The socially conscious minority must act if only to break the vicious circle for the individual who is the product of his environment, and who until then feels unable to break through.

For some of our readers we have wandered a long way from our original theme. To them we can only reply that if they demanded a black and white answer we could have given it in a sentence or two. What we have been trying to do, instead, is to show that considerations of pride, defiance of the powers that be, "victories" and "defeats" are all small, very personal considerations which if we "mean business" should not be allowed to overshadow our objectives which transcend individual considerations without even minimising or sacrificing them. For this reason we would say that the demonstrator who swallows his pride and pays a fine rather than a month or two in prison *and then spends the month or two he would otherwise have spent kicking his heels in prison making propaganda* is, in certain circumstances, serving his cause in the most effective manner. We must be ready to go to prison when we and the comrades whom we esteem consider that our gesture is more effective propaganda than our words. But at all times, if we are serious, such a decision must be taken on tactical grounds first and foremost.

And for the same reasons we believe that we should invite arrest only from a position of strength: of morale, of numbers, of initiative. As to accepting or refusing to be bound over, again we believe that pride should be the last consideration in arriving at our decision. And we would add that we would no more recognise as morally binding a "binding over" order which George Clark could have signed as an alternative to a nine-months prison sentence, than we believe that workers, signing an agreement with their bosses for a pay increase, should respect the "conditions" agreed to by their leaders. *The only agreements which should be respected are made between equals.* To accept imprisonment as the alternative to a binding over order is to abdicate one's chances of breaking that order. (Again we repeat that it would be another matter if for tactical reasons it were thought to be in the interests of the movement to refuse the "binding over order".) But it would take more than the 100-odd demonstrators in prison as we write, indeed it would need the kinds of numbers Kingsley Martin quotes the "anarchists" as considering necessary to put the judicial machinery out of gear, assuming they could be caught unawares.

Where Mr Martin has misinterpreted us, and possibly the Committee of 100 *has* put the cart before the horse, is that we anarchists in fact believe in paralysing the machinery of State *when we are strong enough to do so*, violently or non-violently, depending on the measures the ruling minority takes to protect its positions of power. In the meantime all those who believe in radical social change must propagate their ideas wherever they find an opening, among their workmates, their acquaintances and friends, and, yes, within their family circle. And we must undermine the authority of government by solving more and more of our daily problems ourselves, at district and street, level. And now and then we should give a public demonstration of our unity and strength, by acts of civil disobedience which make the ruling class aware of our growing determination to be rid of them.

(December 23, 1961)

III. OPENNESS OR SECRECY?

The policy of the Committee of 100 has all along been one of non-violence and openness. We now want to discuss the question of openness *versus* secrecy in the light of the Committee's activities and experience in the past year. In general we would say that where it is possible to carry on one's propaganda freely, then secrecy is an unnecessary hindrance, and that the more openly one acts, the greater is the chance of reaching the maximum number of people. At the initial stages of its existence the Committee of 100 depended for its success on its plans for civil disobedient action receiving a maximum of advance publicity; the organs of mass communications were its principal means for reaching the sympathetic minority among the public who would join them in their activities. The question now is whether a point has been reached where a policy of complete openness, so far as action, as distinct from day to day propaganda, is concerned, can only result in one costly "defeat" after another which could in a short time lead to the disintegration of the movement through disillusionment by the feeling that the odds against which we were pitting our forces were overwhelming.

A year ago when the Committee of 100 was formed and its campaign of civil disobedience announced, its potentialities could not be accurately assessed by the authorities. Indeed it will be recalled that at the first sit-down when more than 4,000 people including the "big names" took part, the forces of law and order were content to play the role of onlookers; it is true that they were also faced with an accommodating assembly which packed itself on the pavement and not in the road, around the Ministry of Defence, but they closed an eye to the "obstruction" and there were no arrests. When the second sit-down took place there were as many police as demonstrators, and the arrests started in earnest, and those not arrested were all dragged from the road and dumped on the pavements. By the time the Trafalgar Square demonstration took place (September) the authorities were taking the movement seriously, and operated according to a plan. The demonstrators' chances of achieving their immediate objectives receded into the background. By the time the December demonstration took place not only were the authorities ready to deal with the optimistic plans of the Committee, but they had taken a number of measures such as raiding the offices of the Committee as well as the homes of some of its members; calling on the printers of the Committee's leaflets, arresting five members of the Committee, and charging them under the Official Secrets Act; warning the public that by participating in demonstrations directed at military establishments they were making themselves liable to arrest under these Acts, which carry heavy penalties.

By December 9 then, what free publicity the Committee of 100 had received from the organs of mass communications by its policy of openness on the one hand, can only be properly estimated by considering on the other hand what harmful effect the counter-measures of searches, arrests and intimidation by the police which, of course, were given maximum publicity in the Press, had on many people who were sufficiently sympathetic to the cause but deterred by the barrage of threats by the authorities. And not only were the authorities able to use the weapon of intimidation-through-the-application-of-the-law (even though it is highly questionable whether they will proceed with the charges under the Official Secrets Act, or, if they do, succeed). But by being told beforehand — not to mention the fact that plain-clothes Special Branch officers attend all the meetings of the Committee of 100 where they can not only note the discussions that take place, but single out each individual and form an impression of his views and role in the movement and thus build up a dossier which would be invaluable if and when it was decided by the authorities that the time had come to attempt to destroy this movement — we were saying, that by being told beforehand, the military and civil authorities between them, were able to take all the steps necessary to meet the challenge threatened for the 9th December.

To tell the authorities beforehand that not only are you courting mass arrests, but that those who are arrested have been advised to refuse to give their names because in doing so the machinery of the courts, the prisons, etc., will break down, is a warning as well as an invitation to the authorities to take counter measures to deal with such a situation. Which is what they did. Not only were the barbed wire fences enclosing the air bases strengthened, and patrolled on the ground as well as from the air, but schools were taken over to be used as emergency courts; police were drafted from all parts and the whole operation was carried out with the kind of thoroughness and lack of concern for "expense" which one expects from the authorities when it is a question of defending the sacred "principle" of Authority.

We anarchists would have been most surprised and even disappointed had the authorities acted otherwise. Yes, disappointed because it would have meant that they felt so strong as to be able to ignore the movement of the Committee of 100 completely. The fact that they cannot write-off the movement is the measure of its success after one year of activity. But just because the authorities take the movement seriously it is doubly necessary that the movement should take the authorities seriously. And so far this does not seem to be the case.

In a front page editorial in *Peace News* (December 1) on the police raids on the Committee of 100's offices we read:

> Police brutality and political police are closely related to totalitarian and racist policies; they are also closely connected with preparations for and the waging of war. Elaborate "security" arrangements foster use of underhand devices to weed out spies and enemies of the state. The degree to which any society condones either police violence or the use of political police is symptomatic of the lack of liberty in that society. Political police methods are one of the things we are fighting against.
>
> We believe use of violence and the use of spies, telephone tapping, questioning neighbours (or printers) would all be wrong if used against members of a violent secret political organisation; but at least in this instance they would have some kind of justification. But in the case of the Committee of 100, which has always publicised the names of its members, broadcast its plans to the world and been quite open about its aims and activities, there is no shred of justification.

It is with regret that we find ourselves disagreeing with almost every word of the foregoing paragraphs, especially since *Peace News* is now controlled by the militant elements in the Committee of 100 and not muzzled by a moribund PPU, which values respectability and political orthodoxy as being more important than militancy.

"Police brutality" and "political police" are not phenomena only of those countries pursuing policies which are "totalitarian" or "racial" or which are "preparing for or waging war". They are part and parcel of every State, every nation, in which the latter enjoy privileges connected with power and/or wealth; in which the many depend on the few, whether they call themselves the employers or the State, for their means of livelihood. Police brutality and political police exist in direct ratio to the opposition which the ruling class encounters from those who challenge its authority. Let us be quite clear. The opposition represented by the Labour Party does not threaten the ruling class, the *status quo*. The revolutionary workers' movement in Spain in February 1936, in spite of the victory of the Popular Front parties, did. And for that reason when, only six months later, the military rising was launched, there were as many revolutionary workers in prison under the Popular Front Government as had been liberated in the flush of the Popular Front victory in February. All political parties aspire to the armchairs of government; none challenge the foundations of a society which is maintained by the threat, or use, of force. Indeed, when in office, they use the same machinery to maintain "law and order". Have the editors of *Peace News* read nothing of police brutality in India since independence? Or of the Belgian police during the strikes of last year? to mention only two examples of countries which can hardly be called "totalitarian", "racist" or bent on "waging war".

This naive nonsense about "justification" for phone tapping, snooping, etc., by the police would be laughable if it were not tragic. Here are good, active people willing to suffer imprisonment and forego the temptations of material comfort to achieve a happier world for everybody to live in, who still think that those who are the ruling class will give up their power and privilege without a fight; that in their dealings with those who challenge their authority by openness, non-violence and brotherly love they too will in due course use the same openness, non-violence and brotherly love!

Have they had their illusions shaken by police actions since the raids: by the arrests of their fellow Committeemen under the Official Secrets Act, by the Ambulance trick at the two entrances at Wethersfield and by the arrest of fifteen Marshals at Brize Norton after they had been called by the Police Chiefs "to discuss arrangements" for the demonstration?

If they look upon "openness" as a principle rather than a tactic then it is clear that no examples as to the duplicity of the forces of Authority will influence them. And it would seem that they still consider this question of openness as one of principle as the concluding paragraph from the *Peace News* editorial clearly indicates:

> If the Committee were ever to abandon significantly its policy of non-violence or openness, *then* the police would have some justification for using political police methods, and to the same extent the Committee would itself have compromised democratic and libertarian values. But we now have the right to ask the police not to stoop to underhand, undemocratic and unnecessary measures, and to protest vigorously when they do.

The utter confusion in this kind of thinking is the result of applying the same moral values to the man who is armed with arguments, a desire to see that reason prevails and that all mankind shall live together as equals and at peace, with the man who argues with a truncheon, the majesty of the law, and the threat of imprisonment. Don't our pacifist friends see that in such a relationship the two sides are speaking different languages. That the word justification has one meaning for us and another for them, and that therefore while on the one hand we must expect no consideration from *them*, on the other hand, we are worse than naive if we attempt *to see their point of view*. To say, as does the *Peace News* editorial, that while deprecating political police methods in all circumstances, the authorities would have "some justification" if the Committee were to "abandon significantly its policy of non-violence or openness", is to confer on society, as it is organised today, some kind of *moral right*; or to put it another way, that until we succeed in changing society, what exists is right.

With this view anarchists disagree profoundly. We seek to change society not for the sake of change, but because we believe that the whole edifice of society has been built on wrong foundations. For us it is a question of building on new foundations and for this very reason we do not expect to receive, nor do we ask for, the co-operation of those who are directly engaged in defending the present social edifice from the demolition squads.

At most we shall demand that, since they are the upholders of law and order, they shall not exceed the limits of the powers they enjoy. And not because we are legalists, but because the law is already sufficiently weighted in favour of the *status quo* for the under-privileged majority not to use the law when it is in their favour.

We know that the ruling class can change the law when it does not suit its purpose: as Verwoerd's government is doing in South Africa. But in the meantime it would be, in our opinion, a tactical mistake to allow the authorities, the Press and any other upholders of "law and order" to attack, and inhibit us, by actions which exceed their legal rights.

We must resist the taunts of the gutter press which will be the first to point out that we are opposed to the law yet demand that the police should respect the law. And we must answer them by pointing out that when we break the law we do so for our own reasons, *and knowing what price the law may exact from us in terms of personal liberty*. Because we do not recognise the law does not mean that we recognise the right of the authorities to imprison us without trial.

Neither does it mean that we should allow the police to get away with abuses of their rights, involving violence, or even procedure. They are the "pillars" of law and order; we must insist that they be the first to observe the rules. (Note: the Post Office workers to press their wage demands have not bothered to go on strike. As we write, they are proposing to work to rule. They are not going slow; they are simply carrying out their duties as laid down in the book of words. And just by doing this they will virtually paralyse the postal services. If the public were to demand that the police carry out their duties according to rule the already "undermanned" police force could be made to be even less "efficient" — or should one say "effective"? — than it is at present. Not only would the police be hamstrung, but probably half the population would be on some charge or other and the courts and prisons would certainly be unable to cope with the "criminals".)

The Committee of 100 viewed as a breakaway movement of the CND, that is as a movement which believes that more spectacular methods of propaganda than marches, meetings and parliamentary pressure groups, can result in unilateral disarmament so far as this country is concerned, has achieved all it can achieve, and the leaders of CND far from being embarrassed by its unruly offspring, should be deeply grateful to it. The sit-downs have obviously saved the CND from oblivion and the political pigeon-hole which is the fate of all those movements which delude themselves that they can transform society by influencing political parties, or governments.

The Committee of 100 viewed as a movement which no longer believes in the goodwill of any political party but casts its lot with the people, in the street, in the factory and workshop, is in its infancy — and we say this not disparagingly, but as "brothers in arms", more than anxious that all the positive forces in this movement should be fed, inspired and encouraged, but not sacrificed to a theory or formula. Ideally we must act from strength, in which case we can afford to declare our intentions openly, defiantly. In such a case either we propose to wrest some initiative from government or we are pitting our physical, numerical, social strength against that of authority. But for a movement at present rooted in the coming generation rather than in a section of the working class movement, to our minds, lack of numbers must perforce be counter-balanced by the element of surprise; hence, at this stage the question of secrecy or openness is one of vital importance.

We do not hesitate to advocate that the Committee of 100, as a movement of civil disobedience, should drop its "openness" and seek instead to organise its demonstrations as secretly as it possibly can. Either it is a movement of civil disobedience or it isn't. And if it is, then its aim should be to disorganise the machinery of State as effectively as possible. By informing the authorities of one's intentions beforehand is the most ineffective way of going about it. This, we maintain, is elementary common sense, but only if by civil disobedience one means to change the rules as well as hamper the Government. To advocate new values, a new society, without at the same time doing everything to ensure that there is a breakdown in existing government is as ineffective as seeking to paralyse existing social and economic organisation without having ideas as to what should be put in its place.

The Committee of 100 movement has therefore a double role to play: on the one hand that of propagandists for a libertarian society based on co-operation and equality between men, and the more openly this work can be done the better; on the other hand by acts of disobedience they must demonstrate that Authority is basically weak when faced by even a minority when that minority is united and determined. And to achieve the maximum effect for such activity preparation must be done in secret.

To our minds the most significant social event of 1961 in this country has been the growth of the Committee of 100 movement. 1962 must be a year of consolidation, of growth as a *social movement* which will inspire the working people of this country with an awareness of the real power which now lies dormant in each one of them. No movement of revolt which does not have its roots in the working classes can change society in the direction of freedom; indeed we doubt whether it can change society at all.

(December 30, 1961)

1962-1963

MARCHING ON!

How many people taking part in this year's Aldermaston March entertain hopes that the government will take much notice of their demands? We imagine that the number is not very great. From the point of view of influencing the political parties, one can expect that as the Campaign for Nuclear Disarmament grows so the political parties will manoeuvre to protect themselves from influences which, electorally speaking, would lose them votes.

For the leaders, last year's March was a *triumphal* march, celebrating their first major victory. At Scarborough, the previous October, the Labour Party conference had rejected the Executive's Defence programme and, thanks to the Union bloc-votes, adopted the unilateralists' programme. This was no mean achievement: the next best thing to influencing the Government is to convert the Opposition! But of course, it was all a ghastly mistake. How could the Labour Party offer itself to the country as an alternative government without a Defence programme? Whatever individual members of the party may have thought, it was clear that the National Press would damn the party's chances if the decision were not reversed in time. The ghost of Nye Bevan going naked to the conference tables haunted the Party leaders and the Union executives. The Parliamentary Labour Party almost to a man closed its ranks and inspired by Gaitskell's impassioned rallying call to "Fight, fight, fight!", and the force of the electoral argument, defied Conference decisions.

Between Scarborough and Blackpool Gaitskell succeeded in persuading the Unions to examine their consciences and their policies. "Think — Re-think, Double-Think" and hey presto at Blackpool last October the Scarborough decision was reversed by an overwhelming majority, thanks again to the Trade Union bloc-busters!

And the CND goes marching on. This time perhaps the Canon will have lost his smile of triumph, Jaquetta Hawkes' sombrero will be at a less rakish angle and Michael Foot will be wearing an angry frown.

As a propaganda movement we think there is no doubt that the CND has done very effective work, and the March is good propaganda. As a pressure group it is a flop for all it has with which to press the ruling class are sound arguments and a feeling for human life. Governments have no time for either, and can easily resist both. There are two pressure groups that count so far as governments are concerned; they are, on the one hand the Federation of British Industries and the Bankers, etc., on the other the Trades Unions. Both can, if they have a mind to, make or break governments, because between them they control the nation's economic machine. When they grumble the government has to sit up and take notice. Of course governments have their "arguments" in the shape of the armed and other forces of "law and order"; and they can always count on the support of the Trades Unions when they are at loggerheads with the industrialists and bankers and *vice versa* (e.g. Kennedy's "victory" over the steel barons in America last week). But what can a middle class movement, such as CND, which has declared its political and social impotence by seeking to see its wishes implemented through the normal "constitutional channels" do; what pressures can it exert on government policies?

We are not criticising the CND for not having managed to rid the country of its nuclear armament. We do criticise them for their blinkered approach: of treating what are virtually revolutionary proposals as if they could be dealt with as simple questions of policy, rather like wage restraint, or the decision to tax lollipops. Unilateral disarmament implies that a nation, or a people, are substituting moral values for power values in political relations. This means upsetting the whole economic and social structure; it means an end to privilege, it requires the decentralisation of power, the break-up of pressure groups. In a word it is the social revolution as anarchists understand it. And you cannot legislate for revolution; you have to make it.

Unconsciously perhaps, the frustration which gave rise to the Committee of 100 was the realisation that unilateral disarmament was a proposal so far-reaching that revolutionary and not constitutional methods would be needed to achieve it. The Committee of 100's demonstrations have been valuable in that they have made many people aware of the entrenched power of the State; one hopes that they have also made many aware of the potential power of the people when they know what they want and are themselves prepared to take action to achieve it instead of depending on the right people and the "proper channels".

Let us be both optimistic and without illusions. The revolution cannot be made in a day; individual gestures and self-sacrifice are not enough; the building of a conscious revolutionary movement is an unremitting task, less spectacular for the most part than impressive marches and week-end sit-downs, but in which direct action is the culmination and the consolidation of months or years of preparation. These, it seems to us, are the inescapable lessons for all who want to live in a peaceful world, whether they seek their inspiration in the experience and wisdom of a Gandhi or of a Malatesta.

(April 21, 1962)

ALDERMASTON 1963

What can be hoped for as a result of a successful — as we assume it will be — sixth annual "Aldermaston" march this Easter, can perhaps be assessed by drawing up a balance sheet of what has been achieved by the previous five.

From the point of view of the objectives of the Campaign for Nuclear Disarmament a most eloquent answer is provided in the first paragraph of the editorial in this month's *Sanity* (organ of the CND):

> In case we have forgotten: the twelve months between Easter 1962 and Easter 1963 was the year of resumed nuclear testing, the year of the Cuba crisis and the Indian-Chinese war. It was the year in which the Soviet Union exploded in the upper atmosphere a single nuclear device more than six times greater than all the explosives used in the second world war. It was the year in which Mr Kennedy sanctioned 900 Minuteman missiles, each one with a nuclear warhead capable of an explosive power 100 times greater than the Hiroshima bomb.

It seems clear that the ruling classes of the world are not deterred (or disarmed) by good people tramping 53 miles in their thousands, supported by possibly millions more who will be with them in spirit, even if the few days' respite from life's routine will be spent in other ways.

As a public demonstration; as a gathering of age and youth with the accent on youth, remarkably free from the antagonisms and incompatibility that divide them in Committee, group and branch meetings; as a human protest against barbarity so extreme that atheist and Christian, anarchist and Trotskyist, socialite and socialist, Communist and Conservative, employees and some employers can rub shoulders, tread a common path and share a sausage-roll . . . these are some of the positive aspects of the Aldermaston March. Apart from their attraction *per se*, there is the incalculable, invisible, long-term importance of this confrontation, this "cohabitation" of classes and creeds.

"Aldermaston" attracts this writer too from the purely *organisational* point of view. Many anarchists react to the inhuman over-organisation which characterises the authoritarian society we live in by going to the other extreme, and assuming (or hoping?) that in a free society, because there could be a real community of interests, the day to day affairs of the community could be settled as if by magic, without organisation. This is the dream-world utopia of the individualist, the island inhabited by the smug introvert who believes in the self-sufficiency of the individual as the key to happiness. The reality is that the moment two, let alone 20,000, people decide on common action, they must "organise" their actions. "Aldermaston" is a major feat of organisation, and the fact that it has been so successful so far with a minimum of centralised organisation should be, for anarchists, a source of considerable encouragement. Writing of the second march in 1959, Colin Ward was even then (FREEDOM April 4 1959) drawing attention to the effectiveness of this non-authoritarian form of organisation:

> When you think of the enormous authoritarian structure required to move a regiment of soldiers 50 miles and then think of the limited resources of the organisers of this march, its *ad hoc* system of baggage weapons, despatch riders and support vehicles, and its reliance on the purely moral authority of its marshals over a crowd of people who were the very antithesis of an army, you can imagine what an immense fund of goodwill and responsibility has been drawn from this "unruly mob . . . this rabble" as a correspondent of the *Daily Telegraph* called us, even to the extent, unprecedented in an English crowd, of leaving no litter behind.

The feature of the 1963 March, if one were a hack for our "free" Press, is surely the dust-cart which will bring up the rear of the March. We read this piece of "news", and the organisers' appeal for a "qualified" driver, with pleasure. For even a dust-cart can make some sceptics pause and think.

In the current issue of ANARCHY, one writer (Charles Radcliffe) deplores the fact that CND shows a tendency to becoming a "membership organisation" and "is attempting to get us to march without banners of 'a political nature', and turn us into a liberal-minded procession of lollipop luggers".

That they should be showing a tendency to becoming "a membership organisation" is not surprising. For the first five years of its existence the CND was ignored by the Communist Party of Great Britain; in its fourth year its "respectability" spawned the Committee of 100, an interesting (and valuable) mixture of idealists, exhibitionists and revolutionists.

The fact that the CND in the first *five* years of its existence can boast that its "influence" is expanding whereas the Committee of 100 has enjoyed, by contrast, a short-lived "popularity", could lead one to draw conclusions which, however, do not stand up to analysis.

The CND like all amorphous bodies is the prey of the highly organised, centralised, political minorities such as the Communists and other minority Marxist parties and sects (e.g. Trotskyist. ILP *et alia*). The feature of last year's "Aldermaston" was surely the CP participation. This writer, for the first time (at Aldermaston), had to contend with the "Party" objections to the anarchist case. We can appreciate the alarm in St Paul's as a result of the threatened kiss-of-death from King Street!

The gloomy picture presented by comrade Radcliffe in ANARCHY is justified *only if one ever cherished illusions in the revolutionary potentialities of a body such as the CND.* The Campaign for Nuclear Disarmament has succeeded in expanding in spite of dismal failure so far as its objectives are concerned simply because it advocates the most popular and uncontroversial of all causes and because it seeks to achieve its aim by "respectable" means. It is not surprising if at a certain stage an attempt should be made to discipline it and use it for political ends. Everybody else is having a go, so why shouldn't Canon Collins and his friends?

If the CND is to become effective as well as being impressive, it must either transform itself into a revolutionary movement or enter the political arena as an organised party. Naturally, we anarchists would prefer to see the former happen. The attempt made by the Committee of 100 to do this failed insofar as it resulted not in a revolutionary transformation of the CND but a break-away by the very people who could have been expected to exert a revolutionary influence within the CND. Perhaps they calculated that their "direct action" would galvanise the rank and file of CND into similar action. If so they have, unfortunately, failed. The Committee of 100 is floundering and hoping for an inspired gimmick to catch the headlines once more. The CND remains with its illusions. As *Sanity* puts it:

> This Easter, in 1963, the Aldermaston march and the Campaign for Nuclear

Disarmament want the British government to give Aldermaston and Parliament and all they stand for, which the men and women of this country *made* but cannot *use*, back to the people.

Way back, at the first March in 1958, we quoted from the *Manchester Guardian* the following comment:

> Sprinkled more thickly than report has given out are obstinate ones who insist on thinking. An Oxford undergraduate complained of "All this guff of Britain giving a moral lead". He admits the truth of the "moral stuff — but what we want to know is what political action we can take to change the Government's policy even by a little — and nobody here has said a thing about that".

CND is no nearer to being able to give an answer in 1963 than it was in 1958. It would be churlish to deny that CND has done valuable educational work in making a large number of people aware of the consequences of nuclear war, and persuading them to support any constitutional steps to abolish these weapons. Its failure is that after six years it still talks in these terms:

> Politics begins with something we can *do*. The renunciation of an independent deterrent, and of Britain's part in a NATO deterrent, is something Britain *can* do. It is something which a rapidly growing proportion of the British people — far, far greater than it was when we first marched — think we *should* do. It is something we, collectively, can will to happen *this year*.

CND will still be "willing" things to happen when the British nuclear deterrent will be scrapped by the government as obsolete or impractical. As we write, Mr Wilson, the Labour Party's shadow Prime Minister, has stated in a broadcast to America

> "You are not a military Power if you are dependent on somebody else for your weapons". But Britain could be a very important military Power if she concentrated on conventional forces. Britain's "so-called deterrent" added nothing to the West's strength. What it did was "to use up so much of our resources . . . that we are unable to make an adequate contribution to NATO ground forces in conventional terms.
>
> "If we were to drop this pretence", he said, "of being an independent nuclear Power, we should have more resources in order to strengthen British forces in Germany, to see that they are properly equipped, to see that they are properly mobile and could play a full role in NATO". He was not proposing that Britain should accept the status of a second-rate Power. "We are proposing that we come to terms with the facts of the world".

And when this happens, CND may well try to take the credit, but who is honestly going to fall for that one? Government are not influenced by orderly protests and disciplined marches. The only language they understand and take into account is that of revolution, of direct action which disrupts the economy and upsets the *status quo*. True, they dispose of the force to combat such movements, and it will be pointed out that most times they succeed. But not always.

(April 13, 1963)

RSG-6: FACTS AND OPINIONS

However embarrassing the "Spies for Peace" document may have been to the respectable leaders of the Aldermaston March, they cannot surely overlook the fact that it put the March "on the map", at least so far as the organs of Mass Communications were concerned. "Danger! Official Secret. RSG-6" is a duplicated pamphlet purporting to give details of one of twelve Regional Seats of Government which have been set up throughout the country for use in the event of a nuclear war. Each RSG has "an operational staff of several hundred" headed by top ranking military and civil officers, scientists, medical men and civil servants. No politicians are mentioned. "It is", write the authors of the document, "not a centre for civil defence. It is a centre for *military government*".

Now this pamphlet is a mixture of facts and opinions. Judging by the reaction of the authorities and the Press, it is probable that the facts are true. But the opinions with which the facts are larded seem to us confused, to say the least. The introductory note opens with the following words:

> This pamphlet is about a small group of people who have accepted thermo-nuclear war as a probability, and are consciously and carefully planning for it.

And two paragraphs later we are told that these "professors, top-civil servants, air marshals and policemen" are "quietly waiting for the day the bomb drops, for that will be the day they take over".

Are we to interpret the first paragraph as meaning that this "small group of people" are planning for a thermo-nuclear war in an aggressive sense, are planning *to provoke* such a war? If so, then our second quotation in which it is stated that they are "*quietly waiting* for the day the bomb drops" (our italics) is not indicative of a group of people busily trying to set the world on fire. Is the ambiguity intentional or just a case of slipshod writing?

Let us examine that first paragraph once more. "This pamphlet is about a small group of people who have accepted thermo-nuclear war as a probability". But millions of people in the world share their view. The vast majority feel helpless at doing anything about it and resign themselves to their "fate"; a small minority march, sit-down, protest and resist as best they can. We all know that the "probability" is not removed if this country were to disarm "unilaterally". So long as one power possesses thermo-nuclear weapons the threat of annihilation exists, according to this argument. Would the authors of the pamphlet in such a circumstance consider the fact that "small groups" of people in the various countries "were consciously and carefully planning for it" a sinister move? After all, no one *knows with absolute certainty* what would be the result of a nuclear war (it is not the certainty of annihilation which makes anarchists oppose nuclear war; we also opposed wars when they were fought according to the Queensbury Rules). Indeed, no one really knows for certain whether — or when — there will be a World War III; whether it will be nuclear (mass roasting) or conventional (— more or less — selective roasting); and, of capital importance to the strategists: who will be the "enemy"!

Specialists are boring (as well as "brilliant") people because, apart from the notable exceptions, they eat, breathe, dream and live within the narrow confines of their speciality. RSG-6 is, on the evidence of the pamphlet before us, the dreamchild of such a group of specialists, who wouldn't know how to say boo even to Canon Collins, but who have probably studied Government at LSE, Ballistics at X and Communications at Y, who have been presented with a problem Z to resolve and have produced a "Warren" to which hundreds of "rabbits" have been briefed to scuttle (within four minutes of the warning?) if and when the H-Bombs are delivered. According to the plans provided by the "Spies for Peace" each RSG — or more accurately, RSG-6 — consists of 60 rooms to accommodate and to provide for the domestic needs of this skeleton government. If one believes that nuclear war means annihilation — at least for small countries such as Britain, then the provisions made have a fantastic or macabre ring about them.

The Ministry of Labour is in Room 13, the National Assistance Board in Room 10 is next door to the Messengers (heavenly?). Lavatories in 21 are practically sited next to Ventilating Shaft in 22, while the Treasury (in 15) is optimistically situated next door to that of Power (26). In this surrealist Hades there is a Ministry of Health (30) as well as a Common Services (51). There is, believe it or not, a GPO (to deliver condolences from the dead to the dead?), a Ministry of Labour (provision for the age of Automation? — but what about the markets?), a Ministry of Transport (will the dead bury the dead?), a Ministry of Aviation (in the light of "Honest to God" realism presumably?), a First Aid room (!?), an Information room (a break-through for the Spiritualists?) and a National Insurance room (death benefits, from the womb to the tomb?).

But seriously, Regional Seat of Government 6 is the pathetic product of minds so conditioned to worshipping law and order that they cannot see the futility of Generals without an Army, of Fire Chiefs without Fire brigades, of a Treasury where money has been abolished . . . by H-Bombs; a Ministry of Labour overlording a non-existent labour force; a Ministry of Health attending to the health of the dead and a police force "protecting" non-existent property.

In this respect the pamphlet under review serves a valuable purpose. And those marchers, among them the large anarchist contingent, who "invaded" this rampart of the government of the dead, exposed the waste, the futility, the ridiculous "secrecy" and, to our minds, above all, *the enormous executive powers in the* hands of the permanent officials of State.

RSG-6 *et alia* are the dream children of our rulers in the event of a nuclear war. The anarchists disturbed the respectability of the last day of the Aldermaston March by a symbolic "disturbance". Many of our comrades were arrested. We know only too well that the ruling class will remain unmoved by such demonstrations; they are not meant to move them. Our appeal is to the people in the street, the victims of class and the privileged society. RSG-6 is the ruling class's crash programme in the event of wholesale decimation by H-Bomb warfare but which could also be of valuable service to them in quite a different context, such as a social revolution. But against a determined, revolutionary, responsible people all the police, professors and military will be of no avail. Our task is not to expose *their* secrets (though we have no objection to so doing, given the opportunity) but to help our fellow beings to uncover and realise their own secret ambitions and desires for a happier, richer life. We are educationalists, yes, but also revolutionists. We believe that education and knowledge provide awareness, social consciousness, the desire for freedom. But revolution is the only means towards its achievement.

(April 20, 1963)

REFLECTIONS ON FED 0101

Our first reaction when we read the original Spies for Peace pamphlet was to try and phone up the numbers given therein and see who answered. Who wouldn't? It now appears that a more or less organised campaign of "unauthorised" telephoning has been taking place which in the words of the *Guardian's* Defence correspondent, Clare Hollingworth, is "endangering the efficiency, albeit temporarily, of the British Secret Services". The front-page "revelations" provoked an editorial comment in the best traditions of the gutter press, which the *Guardian* has always been so loud in denouncing.

> This action is not inspired only by misguided idealism. It is outright sabotage. Behind (the idealists) almost certainly stand organisers with a less innocent purpose . . . (with) professional intelligence training . . . Probably someone else has seized on the opportunity presented by the "Spies for Peace" and is doing so with directions from Moscow . . . The majority of CND supporters may feel dismayed to learn of the uses to which their movement is being put, just as most people in Britain will be disgusted by the attempt to sabotage the security services. This kind of action, far from helping towards disarmament, makes it remote.

We would be delighted to feel able to believe that the British Secret Services could be endangered by so simple an expedient as blocking their telephones. Our "respect" for MI5 is not based, however, on a recognition of any superior intelligence among its personnel, but on the almost unlimited financial and technological resources of which they dispose. We have no doubt that as we write these lines, MI5 has already scotched the telephone-blockers, which does not mean that this, in the words of a *Peace News* editorial, "minor guerilla tactic" served no purpose. All actions which help to break down the mystique of an unassailable permanent Authority are valuable and, to our minds, should be supported by anarchist propagandists. And let there be no misunderstanding on this point: on the present scale of activity its value must be assessed as *propaganda*, and for this reason weighed in the balance against efficiency *in terms of propaganda*.

It seems to us that the recent (May 17) *Peace News* editorial "The Telephone Guerillas" and the angry letter it apparently provoked Bertrand Russell to address to the Editor (May 24) — both, incidentally, newsworthy items for the *Guardian* and for obvious reasons — is a case of making a mountain out of a molehill (assuming that it is not just a private war between would-be "leaders" of the peace movement which our spies-for-peace have not told us about). The *Peace News* editorial as a whole deserves the Russell stricture:

> I appreciate that your purpose is to seek personal holiness. No doubt you will all go to heaven. Unfortunately, for us lesser mortals, who have no such hopes, it is not possible to contemplate the prospect as calmly. Personal holiness is an aspiration which has very little to do with either the danger of nuclear war or the possibility of preventing it . . .

On the other hand *Peace News* makes a valid point when it declares:

Over the years the peace movement has been bedevilled by short-term strategies which have put into the background the main task, which is to persuade the majority of people in this country that unilateral disarmament is a realistic policy.

What *Peace News*, unlike a growing number of supporters of the peace movement, cannot, publicly, at least, see, is that not only is unilateral disarmament an *unrealistic* policy, but is also the reason for the "short term strategies" which it now deplores. For years *Peace News* has been warning its readers and supporters that nuclear annihilation is round the corner. It is to the credit of those who have taken them literally that they have done whatever they felt able in an attempt to halt the catastrophe. They have marched, and sat, they have sailed boats and picketed embassies. And if *Peace News* approves when they seek to immobilise airfields or board Polaris submarines, why suddenly get all holier-than-thou when they try to immobilise MI5's telephone network by exercising what Russell calls the "legal right" of any citizen to make a telephone call to the powers that be to find out what "arrangements are being made for their survival"? For those with a sense of humour the "telephone guerillas" have got something. After all, MI5 taps our phones at will; it would be poetic justice if the citizens could return the compliment and block MI5's lines!

But this is the lighter side, yet valuable for all that, of the struggle against Authority. Its value depends on retaining a sense of perspective. There are those in the peace movement who declare that the "spies for peace" should publicly reveal their identity; there are those who believe that by breaking down the whole system of official secrecy one will remove basic causes of war.

One of the valuable aspects from our point of view, and disquieting from that of the authorities, of the Spies for Peace revelations, has been the lack of "leakages" as to the sources of information. We would like to think this indicates a more discriminating, more mature attitude to the problem of secrecy or openness (a subject we were discussing in connection with the sit-downs eighteen months ago). It is on this problem that *Peace News* should be expressing itself and not wasting its precious space on arguments about the pros and cons of revealing *"all* official secrets", which lead nowhere since they are hypothetical questions anyway. If the State apparatus is so undermined that a minority body can have access to all its "secrets", then long before this situation arises all kinds of more important things happen which would make the revelation of "secrets" superfluous.

As we have already indicated, we sympathise with the impatience expressed in the *Peace News* editorial; we disagree, however, with our contemporary as to what are the important issues on which we should all be concentrating our efforts now.

(June 1, 1963)

THE PRESS REVIVES THE ANARCHIST BOGEY

The interest shown by the Press in the anti-nuclear movement as a whole is of quite a different nature now than it was, say, six years ago. Then the Press was prepared to publicise the marches and demonstrations from the "human angle" — sore feet, wet bottoms, long-haired, bearded youths, barefooted, unwashed girls, and so on — and tended to write off any political content the movement might have had. At most they were a nuisance that a "democracy" had to tolerate in its midst. All that has now changed.

The Press now takes a more hostile line, and cannot overlook the possible consequences of the "politicisation" of the movement. And of course they are quite right in sensing a growing maturity in spite of a possible falling off in the number of "activists", and feeling just a little alarmed at what might be the political prospects if the present trend continues. One can expect that the tactic of the Press will therefore be to seek to work up fears of insecurity in the "respectable" middle classes, and to divide the movement loosely joined around the nuclear disarmament movement by scare stories and suggestions that certain "undesirable" elements are infiltrating the movement and driving out the moderate elements. And in this campaign the anarchist bogey will loom large. Already examples of this new line have appeared in the columns of the *Sunday Telegraph* and the *Sunday Times*. The former, which specialises in uncovering Trotskyite conspiracies and the like, published a news item which we reprint in full:

> The Special Branch fears that anarchist extremists acting independently of any organisation will become violent during the official visit of King Paul and Queen Frederika of the Hellenes on July 9-12.
> They know that these extremists will stop at nothing to embarrass the Royal visitors. Demonstrations are being arranged by Earl Russell's "Save Greece Now" committee.
> Support is being given also by the Campaign for Nuclear Disarmament, the Com-

mittee of 100, the League for Democracy in Greece and minority groups from Greek and Cypriot students' organisations. They are all non-violent.

But Mr Michael Harwood, secretary of the London Committee of 100, which is marching from Trafalgar Square to Buckingham Palace led by Lord Russell on the day the King and Queen arrive, believes that there is a danger of violence from unruly elements.

Special Branch men have prepared a report on hooligans who gatecrashed the Aldermaston CND march at Easter.

The Anarchist movement in Britain is non-violent but it is known that there is a minority of dissenters. At present a controversy on the use of force is being carried out in the correspondence columns of the anarchist journal FREEDOM

Note the "anarchist extremists acting independently of any organisation" "who will stop at nothing" "will become violent". They quote Michael Harwood of the Committee of 100 as saying that he believed there was a "danger of violence from unruly elements" and disclose that Special Branch men have prepared a report on "hooligans who gatecrashed the Aldermaston march". This was immediately followed by a reference to the non-violent nature of the anarchist movement in Britain which, however, has a "minority of dissenters". Readers of the *Sunday Telegraph* will put two and two together and conclude that the "unruly elements" and the "hooligans" are in fact this "minority of dissenters".

The *Sunday Telegraph* piece naturally aroused interest in the Press world and specifically in the relationship of the anarchists to the Committee of 100. Our policy on interviews with the Press is to invite them to put their questions in writing and to supply them with written answers. This attempt to avoid misunderstandings and misstatements invariably drives the news-hounds away never to return with their written questions. The *Sunday Times* (complete with photographer) was among them. But this did not prevent them from including the anarchists in the "Focus" feature on the "Mixed-Up World of CND" last Sunday. And who better to quote (or misquote?) than the king-pins of official CND-ism. Thus Canon Collins is quoted as saying that

> As an anarchist fringe has recently been very prominent in the movement the task (of keeping the right kind of balance in CND) is all the more difficult. "Inevitably this means that we sacrifice a good deal of support for what you might call the more normal public".

And Professor Ritchie Calder, vice-chairman of CND who said that he did not approve of widening the movement's terms of reference beyond the nuclear issue, added:

> "Anarchist elements have always been latent — now they are coming out. You've got to remember this generation has strontium in its bones and sputniks in its eyes; older people can't understand."

Calder is also convinced that most of the trouble in Scotland has been caused by a lunatic fringe of anarchists, and not the Communists who have sometimes got the blame. "People do anything under the CND label but here the anarchists are the biggest danger for those of us who want CND to be a protest of decency".

On the other hand, in the section of the "Focus" feature dealing with the Committee of 100 — a mixture of interview and "atmosphere" — the following paragraph is inserted:

> Although the Communist Party has made sporadic attempts to take over both the Committee and CND, the Communist element is thought to be tiny. But there is a wide measure of agreement with the views of the Federation of London Anarchists who crowned the last Aldermaston demonstration by deliberately breaking up the march itself.

Notice again how the "views" (undefined) of the Federation of London Anarchists are linked to their alleged "deliberate breaking up" of the Aldermaston march.

Of course this is the necessary background material from which to draw blood-curdling conclusions and to drive a wedge into this movement of the people which still resists the political parties' kiss of death.

And the *Sunday Times'* conclusions are that "if the tendency to wilder and wilder extremism continues, which seems highly likely" the "influential figures" in the CND may decide that "the time has come to quit". To our minds Canon Collins, like Mr Macmillan, is immune to hints, unpopularity and shoving. He loves his job and the headlines that go with it (and he gets more of them from the CND platform than from the pulpit). And like Mr Macmillan he will not quit so long as he feels he has a mission to fulfil, and a possible clue to what that is may be found in the final paragraphs of this "Focus" investigation on the Mixed-up World of Canon Collins and the other "influential figures" in CND:

> Nuclear disarmers of all shades of opinion agree on one thing — frustration, and hence hasty and extreme action often results from increasing attempts by authority to restrict their protests. Canon Collins, speaking with great passion, should have the last word.
>
> "I think the authorities are mad, quite mad to bottle up this kind of frustration and you can quote me on that. It will only get worse. There's always a risk that in the face of provocation people will despair of democracy".

To the extent that Canon Collins and his friends are in fact the voices of moderation and "protests of decency" one would expect that the tactic of the Press and of reaction would aim at strengthening their hand. The *Sunday Times* piece though not as slighting as the Press has tended to be hitherto does not, in this writer's opinion, do this more than half-heartedly. But perhaps the Press is just slow in changing its line, and that it's only a question of time before

153

they canonise Collins in Fleet Street and witch-hunt the "wild extremists".

(July 13, 1963)

WHAT IS CND FOR?

The reasons given by five leading members of the Campaign for Nuclear Disarmament for refusing to accept nomination for re-election to the National Council — pressure of other work — do not seem to constitute a very strong case for saying, as was to be expected from the national Press, that there is a crisis threatening the existence of CND. As *Peace News*, rightly in our opinion, pointed out in its front page editorial "Is CND Finished?" (September 20), if there is a crisis in CND it is not as some members think a problem of either organisation or leadership.

What, it seems to us, is the attraction of CND is that its local groups enjoy the kind of autonomy which no political party would tolerate, and are as different in composition and activities as are the interests and politics of the people who animate them. It is true, as *Peace News* sadly reflects, that the advances made by the peace movement "have not been very impressive" and that "the momentum of the great protests against nuclear war has declined". Some of us would argue that it was naive to believe, in the first place, that either the peace movement or CND could in fact hope to implement a unilateral, or multilateral, disarmament policy. *Peace News* on the other hand argues that CND "tends to put too much emphasis on the negative side of its work — saying how evil and destructive war is today" while saying very little about "what they are for". And obviously *Peace News* would not be satisfied by the obvious answer: "Why, for peace, of course!" for the problem that needs a positive answer, in our contemporary's view, is "How to deal with conflict, aggression or invasion if it does occur". And if a clear answer to this question is to be found

it will be necessary to go beyond the thinking of all the existing peace organisations.

A further factor points to such a break from tradition. In opposing war the peace movements have often turned a blind eye not only to the danger of aggression, but also to the evils of totalitarianism. They have ignored in sometimes cavalier fashion the human need for some kind of defence and for some kind of political power.

All this is true. But another point which *Peace News* should have added is that in opposing war the peace movements have with few exceptions always turned a blind eye to the institutions of State which depend on violence and various forms of coercion to maintain their authority, power and privileges. But it is clear from the question which our contemporary poses "how to deal with conflict, aggression or invasion *if it does occur*" (the words we have italicised qualify the terms "conflict" and "aggression" and refer not to their daily manifestation within the nation but to war between nations) that either they accept, or they choose to ignore, the basic role violence and coercion play in the regulation of the daily affairs of mankind in authoritarian society — and that means the democracies as well as the dictatorships. For if they did not, then they would have to recognise that war is but one of the weapons in the armoury of authoritarian society. (To bring this "old-fashioned", oft-repeated, observation up-to-date we would add: "and in this age of automation and technology the 'cold-war' is the safety-valve of the capitalist economy"). And in that case war resistance must be seen as one prong in the struggle to undermine the authority, and power of Authority and the State.

But the Law — the judiciary, the police and the prisons — the monetary system, respect for authority, acceptance of the *status quo*, and the rules of the parliamentary circus are, in our opinion, far greater threats to peace than the presence of armed forces and nuclear weapons. They *are* the *raison d'etre* for the armed forces and the threat of war.

The weakness of the *Peace News* approach is its reluctance to face the fact that war is a consequence, not a cause. "For a long time *Peace News* has", we are told

> advocated non-violent resistance as a form of power which can be used as an alternative to military power, as a means of resisting and undermining the organised violence of invasion and of totalitarian regimes . . .
> We believe that if the peace movement does not develop a non-violent defence policy and a new concept of power then it will become politically impotent. For at the present time, while military means of defence are increasingly immoral, destructive and self-defeating, the basic need for defence is perhaps greater than ever.

For those, like ourselves, who cannot follow the subtleties of meaning of that last sentence we quote the concluding paragraph of the editorial:

> This fact underlines the obligation on *Peace News* to present more concisely what is meant by non-violent defence. And it indicates that it may now be necessary to form a new organisation to promote this policy.

Help! Yet another organisation! Randolph Bourne declared that "war is the health of the State". It could well be said that "new organisations are the health of the peace movement". *Peace News* is already darkly hinting at a new organisation to promote a "policy" which so far consists of four words: "non-violent defence policy".

What does *Peace News* really think? What does it mean when it talks of the peace movement developing "a non-violent defence policy"? As we understand it, it means a policy which could be adopted *by governments* as being more effective than one based on nuclear or conventional weapons. This is in fact the Stephen King-Hall line. Is that what they mean? If they mean that defence must pass from the hands of governments (and the military) to the people why don't they say so unequivocally. If the peace movement needs a spring clean in its thinking, let *Peace News*, which is insisting that it does, give a lead by making clear where *it* stands. It accuses the CND leaders of being anxious *not* to have frank discussion on vital topics, yet the front page editorial with its sensational headline is full of riddles worthy of the "New Left" or the Labour Party politicians it attacks.

(September 28, 1963)

1964

CND DOUBLETHINK

When the CND was launched in 1958 its first (and only) chairman, Canon Collins, declared at a Press conference that what they were proposing was "a short, virile and successful campaign to rid Britain of nuclear weapons". CND has done much valuable work in enlightening probably millions of people in this country and throughout the world on the consequences of nuclear war; and has, unwittingly, given birth to all kinds of movements of dissent, the importance of which will probably only be fully appreciated and realised long after CND has ceased to exist. But when all this is said, CND as such has failed as the pressure group it was intended to be. The "short, virile and successful campaign" has become a long drawn-out, impressive but impotent, annual march between Aldermaston and London, a pleasant enough way of spending the Easter holidays in informal and "classless" company, with more than the normal kind of friendliness that one meets, for instance, at meetings of the committed Left. (At least it was, for during the past two marches the participation of, in particular, the Communist Party has deprived it of much of its apolitical spontaneity.)

CND was bound to fail because of the means by which it hoped to achieve its objectives. And after six years it is clear that the leaders have not learned very much, or are unwilling to learn, from their experience. Canon Collins is quoted in last Sunday's *Citizen* as saying

> My own special disappointment is that we are at present exerting little or no political influence.
> CND has to find a way of making politicians take us seriously as a political movement.
> After the second Aldermaston march both sides woke up to the idea that we were a political force and could influence elections. Now they are beginning to doubt that.

To this lament David Boulton, editor of the CND's monthly *Sanity*, added these interesting remarks:

> "This is true. The real division in CND is between long-term and short-term aims.

Some of us want to forge a new kind of political influence for the mid-60s. Canon Collins is more for political expediency."

Not only has Collins not learned very much; he also suffers from wishful thinking when he suggests that the political parties at one stage "woke up to the idea that we were a political force and could influence elections". In this writer's opinion the politicians have paid more attention to The Beatles than they have to CND. (Only last week a with-it Mr Harold Wilson was photographed surrounded by the long-haired Beatles; we have yet to see him in company with the cassocked Canon and a group of *his* long-haired supporters.)

Pressure groups are such by reason of the power they wield over the affairs of the community. The Federation of British Industries (FBI) is a pressure group (some of us think it much more than that) because its policies can have far-reaching results on the lives of millions of workers as well as on the financial situation of the nation. The Trades Unions are, or some might say, could be, a pressure group, because they command the allegiance of key workers who by withdrawing their labour can jeopardise the nation's economy as well as threatening the *status-quo* — that is, the existing set-up which protects the privileged minority and condemns the working, producing majority to subservience, to "second-class citizenship". CND was not a pressure group in this sense because it declared from the outset that it would only play the game according to the rules *laid down by the politicians*. Thus, at the same time, it urged people to think for themselves *and* rely on the wisdom of the politicians to use their power in the interests of the community. The result of this double-think was that the active, thinking members of CND were soon aware of a feeling of frustration so far as means and ends were concerned. The first manifestation — over means — was expressed with the emergence of the *Committee of 100* in 1961, with the sit-down-that-surpassed-all-expectations (the ground for which had been prepared by Swaffham (1959) Harrington (1960) and Foulness (1960)), and in which a group of 100 individuals, including "eminent" citizens supported by nameless thousands considered that the legalistic means to which CND was committed would not receive a hearing in the organs of mass communications. As Bertrand Russell put it in a letter to the Press (February 1961):

We have been driven to a policy of civil disobedience by the lack of representation or the misrepresentation of the policy of unilateralism in the organs of public information. Broadcasting and television are practically closed to us. It is difficult, almost impossible, to get articles or even letters into the daily papers. Most of the press has gone over to Authority — possibly in fear of being otherwise gobbled up.

But Bertrand Russell, as a lifelong believer in government, had no more intention of overthrowing the power structure of society than have Wilson or Khrushchev. Russell's eminence as a mathematician is undisputed; his "eminence" (notoriety) so far as the gutter press is concerned rests on his social background, which contrasts violently with his rationalism, antimilitarism (first world war only) and his attitudes to conventional morality. And we are the first to recognise the importance of his contribution to the breaking down of religious and moral prejudices. But like so many pioneers in the struggle against religious and moral obscurantism, Russell, in politics, is an autocrat, a believer in the most centralised form of government (world government), and therefore clearly, in 1961 when he led the sit-down to Whitehall, at most he had to be considered a reluctant rebel; but never a revolutionary. And those who found themselves seduced by this persuasive and cogent old man may have had their illusions shattered by his "Penguins" on *Has Man a Future?* (his apologia for world government) and *Unarmed Victory* (a pathetic collection of epistolary exchanges which he had with the newsworthy politicians of the day, in a futile attempt to influence them and in the vain hope that his words of conciliation might establish a niche for him in the political annals of our time). The fact is that it was not very long before Russell resigned from the Committee of 100 and the next we heard from him, by way of press hand-outs, were details of the "Bertrand Russell Foundation", a swish set-up with a swish brochure and a sister organisation in the United States, unlimited patronage — financial and political — to ensure its independent existence. Another pressure group with its own potential means of mass communications, research, etc., and prominent among its directors and secretaries, Ralph Schoenman, the man behind the Committee of 100, and Pat Pottle, the man-who-defended-himself at the infamous "Trial of the Six" at the Old Bailey in 1962. (Last week it was announced in the capitalist Press that Pat Pottle had resigned but refused to say why.)

Way back in 1958 we were suggesting that what Mr Priestley and other founders of CND should "investigate more closely" was

why it is that our writers, our philosophers, our scientists and our "intellectuals" with few exceptions make no impact on the public mind when they lend their names to issues affecting the public conscience and the future of mankind.

A question which Mr Priestley (who had a brief flirtation with the "gentle anarchists" but never with the anarchist movement or FREEDOM) did not think worth answering. In 1964 poor Canon Collins bemoans the fact that

CND is too much in the hands of a self-conscious little cadre of intellectuals. People are no longer excited about us. How are we going to sell a new outlook to them?

The answer, a brutal one, is that if Canon Collins wanted publicity he should have boarded Russell's band-wagon (for what it's worth), but that if he, and Russell, really believed that mankind was threatened with annihilation, they should have had the courage and the integrity to advocate drastic measures. Little wonder that the threat of nuclear annihilation has lost its force. For years they have been warning us of imminent disaster, and mankind is still alive on this planet.

(March 28, 1964)

REFLECTIONS ON A COMMITTEE OF 100 STATEMENT

The Committee of 100's Third Policy Statement needs to be examined sympathetically by anarchists even if critically both for the ideas it expresses as well as in respect to the activities it proposes for itself as a movement in the future.

"It is not enough to be merely anti-war". "We have broken with party politics . . . We have ceased to believe in dependence upon representatives and officials". As anarchists we welcome this growing awareness of the relationship of war to social and economic causes, which it has taken the pacifist movement a very long time to come round to, as well as a healthy scepticism regarding politicians and political parties. On the other hand it is clear from the statement that some of our friends are still somewhat muddled in their thinking when, for instance, they also suggest that the "neglected subjects in the twentieth century — problems of violence and its opposite, authoritarianism and its opposite — account very largely for the helplessness of politicians in face of two world wars and the threat of a third".

The Statement also declares that "we are proceeding beyond moral protest — in conflict situations — to take constructive action in their solution". This sounds all very fine on paper, but by what means do they propose to put this action into effect? It seems to this writer that many people in the peace movement have raised the ideas of non-violence, of non-violent direct action, into a sort of religious faith, however much they may deny regarding them "as sectarian doctrines peculilar to ourselves". It seems to us that non-violence *as a dogma* is as stultifying to revolutionary thinking as is violence. As propagandists our principle function should be to seek to awaken a social conscience, as well as a desire to act, among as many people as possible. The fact is that no lasting radical changes will ever take place until there are a very large number of people wanting, and working, to effect such changes. As to how these changes will came about will depend on a whole number of circumstances which those concerned in the struggle at the time will have to deal with to the best of their abilities. To state now as a dogma that whatever is achieved must be achieved by non-violent (or, for that matter, violent) methods condemns a movement to sterility. What we need to examine, and to make people aware of, are the forces opposed to change; why they are opposed and how they protect themselves. Each individual must then decide for himself which of the means available to him he is prepared to use in the event of a "confrontation".

On the organisational level the Statement declares:

"We look forward to better and closer relations with all other organisations and individuals of the independent peace movement. We propose joint discussions, projects and demonstrations in which people of different persuasions can participate in their different ways without prejudice to their own values or to our common objectives".

In the public mind the Committee of 100 is the highly successful, much publicised sit-down movement which broke away from the more respectable parent body, the CND. As such it has done its job, has inspired a number of people and has taught us many lessons for which the anarchists are the first to express their gratitude. But we would suggest now that the Committee of 100, as such, has exhausted its possibilities, for we get the impression that what is left are a number of well meaning individuals in search of a *raison d'etre*. This desire to keep it alive at all costs, does more harm than good to the image, the impact, of the Committee in its heyday.

That it failed to rouse the people of this country to take direct action against nuclear armaments is of no importance except possibly for the very few people who believed this could be achieved. That it failed to snowball after a brilliant start may or may not have been due to shortcomings in one or more aspects of organisation (the detailed lessons of the sit-down movement have still to be discussed and digested), or in the personalities directing the movement, or in the excessive sacrifices demanded from those willing to participate in the sit-downs. With all its shortcomings the Committee of 100 obviously inspired many peopled to come out of their shells and challenge authority, and its success was brief but brilliant.

However successful it might have been it could not have continued indefinitely, and in our opinion, those who now seek to revive the Committee are doomed to failure because such movements, by their very nature, must have a limited existence, as well as limited scope.

We humbly suggest to those activists in the Committee of 100, who have learned from their experience that "to merely be anti-war" is not enough, that what is needed is "new thinking and action about education, housing, health, communications, transport and industrial relations"; that "party politics" and "dependence upon representatives and officials" is not for them and that what is needed are "new experiments in regional, local and functional administration in which the importance of the individual counts more than the importance of 'the machine' ", that they should ask themselves whether they would not serve their ends and further their cause better by working with the anarchists who have been, after all, advocating and propagating these ideas for a very long time!

(August 22, 1964)

1981

AFTERWORD by Gillian Fleming

According to *The Cap of Liberty* there were 300,000 marchers. It was an exuberant and triumphal affair. Green flags (borne by Irishmen) demanded universal, civil and religious liberty. White flags demanded trial by jury. Red flags demanded liberty or death. Sky blue flags demanded a free press. The various Committees carried white wands with knots of red riband and large branches of oak and poplar so that they "gave no faint idea of the approach of Birnam wood to Dunsinane". A large terrier with a universal suffrage badge also wore a white collar with a red riband on both sides, on which were inscribed the words "No dog tax!" All was decorum and good nature, with plenty of music, despite the small pieces of black crepe fastened to most flags in memory of the Peterloo massacre. Whenever a deviation from the line occurred there were cries of "Order!"

One hundred and sixty one years divide this early Chartist demonstration from the CND march in London in October 1980, which was, incidentally, attended by far less people. Yet how striking the basic similarity between the one and what we could see with our own eyes of the other! Here again, the colourful flags and banners, proclaiming under the umbrella of the bomb a multitude of causes; here again the large and the little dogs, with their CND badges this time, the jolly bands, the marshals keeping order, the predominantly day-tripping sense of fun — to which the small group of historians demanding a "continuous supply of history" adds a suggestion of black humour. And finally here again are that dying, but still dangerous breed, the politicians, with their familiar and falsely comforting speeches.

So, have we learned anything over the last century, let alone over the last decade? An article published in FREEDOM on the eve of the 1980 march, entitled 'The Old and the New' definitely thought so. It expressed the belief that people are much less naive this time round. They are aware that elections and demonstrations (even, one presumes, the dramatic battles in Brokdorf, north-west Germany, between anarchists and 'undogmatic' groups on one hand

and police on the other) change nothing. Law no longer frightens as it did, nor big names impress. The issue of violence *v.* non-violent is less important, as it must be. Because everything has become more urgent.

Indeed, there can be no question of this. FREEDOM articles here express scepticism about the imminence, or probability, of nuclear war and (rightly) castigate CND's leadership for *alarming* people into their cause. But MAD is no longer the undisputed doctrine of the military apparat. From the Pentagon has come the concept of limited nuclear war with Europe as its 'theatre'. Despite the simple wrongness of the notion that such war could ever be confined to certain designated areas of the planet it has become luminously clear that an influential section of the western war machine (and war-studying intelligentsia) believe that, in the advent of a nuclear attack, large parts of America could survive unscathed. At the same time efforts are being made to make nuclear war seem, as it were, more normal. While the Conservative government is about to launch a campaign justifying the build-up of nuclear weapons, there has been a recent upsurge in talk of civil defence and the need for greater preparation, as if this were quite a feasible proposition. On another level, and over a longer time, but more evident since the Vietnam war, there has been a consistent process of perversion of our culture through distortion of language. This, as E.P. Thompson has pointed out, "makes possible a disjunction between the rationality and moral sensibility of individual men and women and the effective political and military process". Such a 'disjunction' helps to prepare for war. And "wars commence in our culture first of all".

What Thompson did not, but could well have added (and his omission is of relevance to the anarchist point) is that our culture is so utterly permeated with the values of the military/political/industrial castes which constitute the State that rules us, and which largely depend for their existence on the threat of war, that their role is scarcely ever questioned. As Herbert Read wrote just after the last world war, and as this volume reminds us: "Government is force; force is repression, and repression leads to a reaction, or to a *psychosis of power* (my emphasis) which in turn involves the individual in destruction and the nations in war. War will exist as long as the State exists".

Bearing in mind such considerations have we time, as 'The Old and the New' article puts it, to worry about *a* movement as opposed to movement itself against death?

I am, perhaps, a little more doubtful than the author of that article that despite the urgency, the lessons have been learned this time round; hence, to my mind, the vital importance of this book. Essentially it is a handbook for those already involved in the struggle of which CND forms — or should form — only a part. It is a handbook which, above all, and for excellent reasons, warns against *a* movement — whether it be a revitalised CND, resuscitated Committee of 100 or the new Anti-Nuclear Campaign.

It is too early to know whether this latter body, which has arisen with the development of the opposition to nuclear energy, will manage to institutionalise and tame it, and in so doing kiss it to death. Many anti-nuclear groups in any case, while they may criticise ANC, are mere talking shops. Direct action groups such as the Torness Public Parks Department or the militants who last year blocked a British Rail goods train carrying nuclear waste for dumping in the sea are fighting a very lonely battle. They lack active support from their own comrades.

What is needed is the fusion, or closer association of groups fighting nuclear energy with those fighting war. This will broaden perspectives and the propaganda will better reflect, as it has to do, the inseparable links between war, capitalist economies (of all kinds) and the destruction of the world's delicate ecosystems.

What is needed is a sustained *guerrilla* campaign, independent of CND, ANC or any other such movement; a guerrilla campaign in the sense of a series of autonomously organised offences carried out by individual groups, whether these involve controlled sabotage of property, occupations of armament factories, disruption of key communications and transport, leafletting or picketing of workers in the 'defence' and nuclear industries, or whatever.

Though we are nearer to war since CND first hit the road, such actions cannot be dismissed as mere Quixotic gestures. Over the last few years we have seen the struggle of workers in such companies as Aerospace, Vickers, Rolls Royce, BAC and Parsons to convert — at least partially — from arms manufacture to socially useful production. There is no reason why the struggle should not spread. But it would spread much faster were the workers (and indeed, why not those bureaucrats who were recently on strike, and thereby knowingly disrupting signals intelligence stations and defence establishments?) to be faced regularly with the arguments which this book — uniquely so far — provides for us.

That its message is as topical and important today as yesterday is shown by the fact that even some who would regard themselves as 'libertarians' are still anxious to separate their broader political stance from their nuclear disarming. A recent article in *Peace News* states, for example, that

". . . as campaigners for nuclear disarmament (and not as anarchists or pacifists) we should chiefly look to civil disobedience for its *strategic use*. We should only make it a *secondary* aim of our actions to use civil disobedience as a proto-political form for the cultivation of a libertarian, anti-state society."

Thus, he suggests, "we should call ourselves dissidents" and "our main actions should be in central London — seat of political and media power and maximally disruptive".

Protest without Illusions stands at the opposite end of this argument. It is illusion indeed to believe that sitting down in Whitehall or "encircling and weaving threads symbolically across entrances of key institutions (e.g. Ministry of Defence, Cabinet Office, Parliament)" as this same author favours, will shift even one tiny political mind in the direction of sweet reason. It is folly to believe that our energies would be better spent in central London, addressing politicians and journalists, than at the factories and bases, the nuclear sites and power stations. It is obscurantism to proclaim that we are 'dissidents' (what does this mean?) when we should be declaring and explaining our specific anti-statism and anti-militarism. It is certain death to see anarchism as but the twirly bit on the temple of nuclear disarmament.

Nuclear arms cannot be de-invented. They have become an integral part of the war machine. To believe that they could be removed from the arsenal because they're not nice, while leaving the arsenal itself intact, or that statecraft can be played at without generating the psychosis of power which Read described, is to think in fragments when now, more than at any time, we must think in wholes. Not Cruise missiles but war itself must be our target and with it, the class-based, power-centred institutions which ferment it.

We have no secondary aims.

London March 1981   **G.F.**

INDEX

Aldermaston Marches 92, 1958 15, 1959 35, 1960 67, 1961 93, 1962 140, 1963 142, 146
ALLAUN, Frank 37
anarchists and the Law 137
anarchy 42, 129
Arrests at Sit-Downs 97, 123, 126, 131
Atom Plants 1
ATTLEE, C. 4

BACKERT, Prof E.M. 24, 26-27
BERNERI, Marie Louise 43
Bertrand Russell Foundation 159
BEVAN, Aneurin 4, 38, 48, 90, 140
Blue Streak Missiles 70-72
Bogeys, Communist 59, Trotskyist 151, Anarchist 151-154
Botulinus Toxin 24
BOULTON, D. (Ed. *Sanity*) 157-8
BOURNE, Randolph 155-6
BROCK, Hugh (Edc. *Peace News*) 21
BROCKWAY, Fenner 37, 117
BROWN, George 70
BUTLER, R.A. (Home Secretary) 98, 102, 117

CALDER, Ritchie on anarchists 152
China 54, 62
CHISHOLM, Dr Brock 25, 26
CHURCHILL, W.S. 4, 60, 115
CLARK, George 117-119, 131
CND Bulletin, 35, 36
CND Leadership crisis 154
COLLINS, Canon John 13, 14, 42, 89, 94, 144, 153, 157-8, on anarchist "extremists" 152, on intellectuals 160
Colonialism 47, 65
COMFORT, Dr Alex 12
Committee of 100, on Berlin "crisis" 107, as propagandists 139, Third policy Statement 160
Common Market 61
Communists 93, 95, 144, 153 — bogey 59
Conscription under Lab. Govt 71
CROSSMAN, Richard 104

DAY, Alan 46
Defence White Paper 1960 66
Defence Debate, Commons 1955 4; Lords 1959 31; Lab. Conf 1960 79-80
Direct Action Committee (DAC) 21, 35, 38-39, 123

Economy, Permanent War 47
EISENHOWER, Gen Ike 52, 60, 62

FARLEY, Christopher 21
F.B.I. (now CBI) 141, 158
FOOT, Michael 21, 56, 104, 140
Four-minute Warning 72
FREEDMAN, Max (journalist) 53-54, 57

GAITSKELL, Hugh 104, 140
GALE, John (journalist) 16
GAULLE, Gen. de 48, 50, 56-57, 61, 63
Germany, West. Economic recovery 61

HADLEY, A. (author) 109
HART, Capt. Liddell (military writer) 5
HARWOOD, Michael 152
"Has Man a Future" 159
HAWKES, Jacquetta (CND) 140
HEALEY, Denis 6
HOLLINGWORTH, Clare (journalist) 149
HOME, Lord 114
HUGHES, Emrys (Lab. MP)

"Infantile Leftism" 128
Intellectuals 82, 131, 159-160
Irrationality, War and 115

KENNAN, George 58
KENNEDY, John 58, 141
KHRUSHCHEV, N. 52-59, 62, 114, 115, 159
KING, Cecil (Press baron) 85
KING-HALL, Stephen 88, 156

Labour Party, & German rearmament 77; disunity 78, conference 1961 140; H-bomb Campaign Cttee 7
LEVY, Ben 37
LLOYD, Selwyn 52

Macmillan, Harold 62, 106, 114, 153
MALATESTA, Errico (anarchist propagandist) 131, 142
MARTIN, Kingsley 90, 127, 129; on anarchists 128, 132

Media (see also Press) 114, 134
Medical Research Council 49
M.I.5 149
MILLIS, Walter (writer) 13
MONNET, Jean 61

Nat. Council for Abolition of Nuclear Weapon Tests 7
Nation's Safety & Arms Control 109
Nationalism 65
New Statesman 21; on Civil Disobedience 86-87
NKRUMAH 65
NOEL-BAKER, Philip 54

Official Secrets Act 133, 134
OTTER, Laurens 28-30

PADLEY, Walter (Lab. MP former ILPer) 104
Peace News (PPU organ) on police raids 135, on openness 136, on "telephone guerrillas" 149-50; on non-violent resistance 155
Peace Pledge, The 69
Personalities, The Media & 114, 124
Phone tapping 136, 148-50
Pickenham, North demo 38-39
Picketing of war factories 81
Polaris bases 84, 87
Police brutality 135-136
POTTLE, Pat 159
Power struggle 65, 112
Press (see also *Media, Bogeys*) 106-107; and the Marches 80, 82, 93, 151; and sit-downs 85-86, 96-97, 120, 123
PRIESTLEY, J.B. 7, 8, 10, 90, 159-160
PRATT, David (English farmer & would-be assassin of S.A. Premier Dr Verwoed) 102
Pravda 107
Pressure Groups 158
Privilege 113
Publicity for demonstrations 100, 128

RADCLIFFE, Charles 143-144
Rand Corporation (USA) 48
RANDLE, Michael 21, 84, 96; on civil disobedience 101, 103
REID, Bruce 116
READ, Herbert 81-82
R.S.G. (Regional Seats of Government) 146-148

RUSSELL, Bertrand 7, 8, 10, 20, 69, 85-86, 105-106, 125, 151, 159; on direct action 19, 75, 79; Lords Debate 32-34, 40; on non-violent demos 80; on sit-downs 86, 158-159
Russian armament 63

SANDYS, Duncan 57
Sanity (organ of CND) 144-145; on objectives 142
SCHOENMAN, Ralph 117-119, 159
SCOTT, Rev Michael 79, 86
SEATON, R.E. 117-119
SIMON, Lord 31, 33
Sit-Down Demonstrations: Feb '61 84-85, April '61 95, Sept '61 107, 133, Dec '61 120-122, 133, 134, Brize Norton 136; costs 102
Socialist Leader (ILP organ) 20
"solid majority" 130-131
Sorenson, Rev R. 37
Spain 1936 135-136
Special Branch 116, 134
"Spies for Peace" 146-148
STALIN, J. 1, 112
Steel production, European 61
STRACHEY, John 5, 72-74
Strike Weapon 130
Swaffham demonstrations 19, 21

TAYLOR, Prof A.J.P. 90
THOREAU, D. 131
TITO, Marshall 59
Tribune 86, on civil disobedience 87, 100, 128
T.U.C. 49, 141

ULOTH, Arthur 112-116
"Unarmed Victory" 159

Voters' Veto 37, 39, 68

WARD, Colin on organisation of marches 143
WATKINSON (now Lord) 70
WILLIAMS, Len 76
WILSON, Harold 158, 159; on Brit. military power 145
Work to Rule 137

YATES, Victor (Lab. MP) 37

ZUCKERT, E. on accidental missile launchings 109